Endorsements

Writing in the tradition of griots, African wisdom keepers and storytellers, Dr. Mapp's latest book, *Making Sense of Today,* provides a resource book for navigating the 21st century with a special focus on continuous learning and relationships. ...Her new book broadens our scope to how we interact with and make sense of the larger global society. ...Dr. Mapp provides us with our own personal guidebook for how to be the change we seek in the world.

This book is for people of all ages and ethnicities and provides insight into the various pathways of how to live life fully and responsibly with meaning and purpose. ... More than ever, what people need now are principles to live by, ways of interacting and ways to live that make sense of how to live a life that sustains the family, the community and the environment. So it makes perfect sense to get a copy of Dr. Mapp's new book   --   \
-- Jim Embry, Sustainable Communities Network

Making Sense of Today ... is a self-help book that is designed to help the readers cope with where they are today and make a plan for tomorrow. ... Everything is connected and affects other things that happen next. ...This book was very well organized. It begins with what is needed to make sense: to evaluate the past and make a plan to move forward. The author then delves into the current world, revolving around how there are so many opinions, but when you stop, think, and listen, people may find they share similar life experiences. The author concludes this book by demonstrating how schooling and quality of life are intertwined and that both are needed for ...success....

There are many points the author brings up in this book, but she always goes back to three: 1) making decisions and making choices; 2) continuous learning, and 3) positive relationships. My favorite part of this book was how the author included questions at the end of every chapter for the reader to go back and evaluate themselves to see where they are and what they need to improve ...

...I liked how the author did not use difficult terminology or concepts to get her point across. It made the book more enjoyable because it did not feel like the author was talking down to the reader; she was simply sharing thoughts and ideas. In fact, there was nothing I disliked about this book. I would rate this book **4 out of 4 stars**. .... I would recommend this book to anyone who wants to evaluate their life and make some changes going forward.
—Rachel S.1, Official OnlineBookClub.org review (posted 24 Dec 2021).

MAKING SENSE OF TODAY FOR BETTER CONNECTIONS TOMORROW
(2ⁿᵈ ed., Vol. 1 © 2020)
and
MY CHILD, OUR FUTURE
(2ⁿᵈ ed., Vol. 2 © 2021)
Are Excerpted with 2023 Updates from the Following Earlier Editions

YOU ARE YOUR CHILD'S BEST TEACHER:
A Holistic Guide to Link Home and School © 2015
First Edition

You Are Your Child's Best Teacher: A Holistic Guide to Link Home and School © 2015 is an outstanding contribution. It is a timely and useful guide for parents, teachers and all involved in helping children and young people develop and prepare to become successful adults. … Using her holistic perspective…she has provided us with very important and useful insights. The book enables parents in particular to think and plan to support the development of their children from birth to maturity, through school and the workforce. It is written as only a parent, teacher and counselor could– comprehensive, easy to read, but thoughtful and very, very useful!
--James P. Comer, M.D., Yale Child Study Center, Maurice Falk Professor of Child and Associate Dean, Yale School of Medicine.

International Book Endorsements

Just want to let you know that I have completely read your *Holistic Guide*… although it is designed for U.S. families, adults and parents, … I think the Guide is universally relevant and helpful for all countries & peoples. …Your Guide is insightful, and from personal knowledge, experience and observation, problems identified with the public education system from the 1940's (my generation) through to now, also exist in countries that imported Britain's education system. However, many factors as you have listed, have contributed to poor education outcomes wherever the model was introduced. I hope your Guide is widely accepted and used in Homes and Schools throughout U.S.A., so that people at all levels and the electorate are truly educated, informed and can be responsible adults.   *-- Cheers! Jeanne C., Canada*

In separate informal conversations about the book, a *tech in India* and a *salesperson from Kenya* asked if the books were available in other countries since parents need help with today's children of various income levels.

OUR CHILDREN AND FUTURE
Lessons in Family and School Engagement © 2019
Second Edition

Our Children and Future is an excellent book for parents, teachers and all those concerned about the development of children. The book challenges the reader to move into the 21st century on child development. -- *Dr. Jawanza Kunjufu, author of* **Raising Black Boys** *and* **Raising Black Girls.**

Impressively and exceptionally well written, organized, and presented, *Our Children and Future: Lessons in Family and School Engagement* (2019) by Dr. DeBora Mapp is extraordinarily innovative, 'real world practical' in application, and an ultimately inspiring read for parents, teachers and other caregivers seeking to prepare children of all ages and backgrounds to have and hone the life skills necessary to deal with whatever the future presents to them. *Our Children and Future* is unreservedly endorsed and recommended for personal, professional, community, and academic library collections. — *The Bookshelf of Margaret Lane, James A. Cox, Editor-in-Chief, 2019 Midwest Book Review*

Our Children and Future is a welcome resource for parents who are overwhelmed or just looking for directions to link home and school. I often write of **The Power of One** to change issues in society. Dr. Mapp addresses the four challenges that I research and believe that we need to address to establish relationships with our students and our schools: communication, collaboration, culture and caring....

Dr. Mapp's book offers a step-by-step guidebook to bridging home and school issues that are age, grade, community, and culture sensitive and specific. Her practical strategies, based on research and reality, offer hope and suggestions on how you can prepare your child for 21st century challenges and opportunities. --*Dr. Stephen Sroka, Adj. Asst. Prof., Case Western Reserve, Pres. Health Education Consultants, Dr. StephenSroka.com.drssroka @ aol.com*

The SAUCE Series

MAKING SENSE
of
TODAY
For
BETTER
CONNECTIONS
TOMORROW

(2nd ed., Vol. 1)

DeBora L'T. Mapp, EdD

We're All in this Together for
the Good of Our Children and Nation!

MAKING SENSE OF TODAY
FOR BETTER CONNECTIONS TOMORROW (2nd ed., Vol. 1)
Copyright © 2020 by DeBora L'T. Mapp, EdD

Published by Inspired Schooling Solutions Publishing
P.O. Box 802, Louisville KY 40203-0802

All rights reserved. No part of this book may be reproduced, stored or transmitted without the written permission of the author, except for the inclusion of brief quotations or in a review.

This volume was updated in 2023 with outcomes from the viral and social pandemics. This volume includes excerpts from the original 2nd Edition: *Our Children and Future: Lessons in Family and School Engagement* © 2019.

Limit of Liability/Disclaimer of Warranty: The author makes no warranties or representations with respect to the completeness of the contents of this book that introduces many topics, and specifically disclaims any implied warranties or fitness for a particular purpose. The clues and strategies in this guidebook may not be suitable for your situation. Dr. Mapp is not a counselor and professionals should be consulted when appropriate. She also assumes no liability for the possible good things that may happen to you, your families or communities because of information from this book.

Because of the dynamic nature of the internet, any web addresses or links in this book may have changed since publication and may no longer be valid.

Making Sense of Today for Better Connections Tomorrow
(2nd ed., Vol. 1)
DeBora L'T. Mapp, EdD   Copyright © 2020
ISBN-13:   978-0-9971310-6-2   Print Paperback
ISBN-13:   978-1-312-01623-1   Lulu Imprint E-Book

Printed in the United States of America

This book and S.A.U.C.E. Series

THE **SERIES**

Speak and **A**ct on **U**nspoken **C**onnections to **E**mbrace Change

are dedicated to the peoples before us who gave so much:
my ancestors and beloved parents
who are no longer with us;
and my seven siblings, five children, seven grandchildren
and our large extended family and friends!

May this book be useful in giving its readers
the will, strength, courage and commitment
to do what's necessary
to make sense of today
so we're ready to think critically,
feel, speak and act on the unspoken and unseen,
to meet opportunities
and solve complex problems challenging
our 21st century global world!

With God's help
and the convergence of our wills,
we can and will
get this right!

Peace, Love, Hope, Courage, Joy and Light!

Acknowledgements

Before writing my first book, I was challenged by a young man at a New Jersey conference who told me that I needed to share what I knew with other people. I'd like to thank him and my sister, Angela, who told me that the four sheets of parent tips I developed for our church's back to school family ministry should be developed into a 40-page booklet, entitled *You Are Your Child's Best Teacher: Intentionally Linking Home and School* © 2012.

I was told by Msiba and Chester when I presented the booklet at a workshop that I needed to add more of what my former husband, Jim, and I did in rearing our children, which became the first edition © 2015. Thanks go to them for decades of friendship and their reminder of the decade of learning from Jimmy and Grace Boggs (Boggs Center to Nurture Community) that shifted our status quo. Studying with them built connections between dialectics and change that required a holistic stance since life and learning are layered and complex.

My children and siblings listened and offered suggestions. Ayodele also offered computer and technical advice. Siku, Ava, Jon, Obiora and Angela helped with the first cover and my children and siblings, Toney, Brenda, Jim and Angela helped me rename the newest version. Segun, Brenda, Toney, Mrs. Bettye and other family members offered words of encouragement and critiques, suggestions or school issues. Thanks to Nancy D. for the final edit.

Thanks go to Zariah and her first cousins for input with the student piece, Maisha for writing her first book, and to my other grandchildren for being my writing inspirations. My Daddy, Ivy, my youngest sister, and my twin sons, Irucka and Obiora, authored their first books over the years. Mama started me on my doctoral journey and Zariah, my oldest grandchild, kept asking me when I would finish. Memories of Mama and Daddy were with me.

My first mentor, George the BeeTV, helped with my business acumen. Janel the editor helped in clarifying my writing. I'd like to thank the many people whose brief quotes I used within the book that gave added substance. Learn more about them and their links to families, schools and national concerns on the internet or in articles and books from your local library.

I'd like to acknowledge the many community folk and parents I met over the years as I volunteered, worked with them and/or taught their children. I learned something from all of them and all my students. I struggled to make this book useful for the good of all our children, but especially our Black children, our families and schools, communities and ultimately, nation and world!

Finally, I thank you, God, for all the above! Asante sana!

Table of Contents

They who dwell in the ends of the earth
stand in awe of Your signs.
You make the dawn and the sunset shout for joy.
—*Psalm 65:8*

Introduction

In this period of rapid change and uncertainty, people everywhere are trying to make sense of the challenges and changes that threaten families, employment, housing, health, education, and the earth. Technology has enabled us to connect with others, but we must balance its material wonders with the spiritual demands of our human nature. Change is needed to overcome challenges and to meet opportunities of the viral pandemic and long-standing social pandemics. It's possible when we Speak and Act on generally Unspoken but Connected topics so we can Embrace change.

We must learn to balance the material wonders of technology with the spiritual demands of our human nature.
—*John Naisbitt and Patricia Aburdene*

Making sense requires understanding the deeper levels of people's needs, including emotional well-being, love and belonging, safety and security, and physiological needs. All these needs are threatened during this period and technology adds to these threats. Families, as the smallest social units in society, have a crucial role in socializing and protecting children's well-being, allowing them to contribute to society. Wise and practical strategies are needed to navigate through the many challenges and problems families face. This can't be done in isolation because everything is connected.

When sense is made, better choices and connections will hopefully be made to improve life. Some people progress easily while others seem stuck in the past when family and national history are not examined. The world continues to shrink in ways never imagined through technology and individual reactions can influence and impact humanity and the world today.

The world is filled with different races and cultures, and in the United States, we have a tendency to be biased against difference. We have to respect cultural, religious and racial differences, no matter our political leanings. Respecting others begins with a self-awareness that no culture is more valuable nor correct than any other culture. For the self-preservation of people and our earth, we have to respect and build positive relationships.

…we have overreacting politicians blowing smoke, cloaking the real issues facing America, and stoking anger for political gain.
—*Principle Based Politics.org*

Making sense begins with how people are reared in their families of origin and the communities around them. As the smallest social units in society, families are not just collections of related adults and children, but they are institutions like education, religion, economics and government. Families, like other institutions, are important to the survival and functioning of society. They have the common purpose of controlling the behavior and expectations of individuals in a nation. Families help socialize and protect children's well-being, so children, in turn, become capable of contributing to society. Families need to continually learn, and formal education continues the process of learning that begins with families.

Adults have to work on many levels to support their families while keeping our democracy and society running – within a global arena. Everything is connected and sense is needed so people can continue to live and thrive, not just survive. These connections occur on multiple "pasenture" (past, present and future) levels. This book helps in this regard. Wise and practical strategies are offered as clues to help resolve problems and challenges as historical and contemporary connections are made to families and learning.

The twenty-twenties are special. Years like 2020, with the first two digits matching the second two, only happen once in a century. Spiritually, some think that the number alerts people to be prepared mentally and physically for change. 20 two times is 40 or 20 doubled is 40. In numerology, the theme for 2020 is building solid foundations while working on exceptional change in our modern world. The number 40 is significant in many cultures and religions.

In the Christian Bible, the number 40 is used for important time periods or significant amounts of something and is mentioned more than 140 times. In the Quran 40 is mentioned 4 times in important events. In Sacred Scripture, 40 means new life or growth, transformation and a change in great tasks. In Hebrew, one source mentioned that it's a year to Widen Your Mouth in Wisdom or Zip It Shut. Chinese beliefs in Confucius are increasing.

Other facts about 40: Forty is the only number in English with letters in alphabetical order. 40 below is the only temperature that is the same in both Fahrenheit and Celsius. Ships during the bubonic plague in Europe were isolated for 40 days before passengers could embark. The word quarantine came from the Italian 40 or quaranta. Women are pregnant for 40 weeks and the standard American work week is 40 hours. Anyone can add their birth year and the age they'll be or were in 2020 to get the same answer. Try it for fun!

The STATUS QUO | New Life > / < Old Life | CHANGE

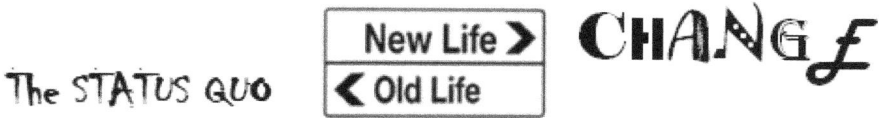

Change is the only thing that's constant in life and that was shown again and again in the early 2020s. Whether you believe that the virus pandemic happened in a divine scheme by God or Mother Nature to get our attention or was laboratory manufactured, the early 2020s has been a surreal or unreal period occurring all over the world at a rapid pace. It's different from the 1918 pandemic due to technology that allowed everybody to know all the details in real time rather than reading about it in the newspaper in the future.

But...it's important to know who disseminates the information to determine if it is really true (check SNOPES) or just sensationalism to get people to react as harshly as possible. It's amazing – people can view the same video or picture but interpret it through their own lens as to whether it's true or not. How confusing for young people looking at some adults on screens or even at home who seem to want to disrupt their future lives.

It's 2023 and studies are still trying to determine what really happened during the beginnings of the viral pandemic. But we do know that there were more deaths in our nation than occurred in all the other countries in the world. The deaths really caused a collective grieving that is still not resolved when looking at the harsh reactions to life in general today. With the loss of so many lives due to the viral pandemic, more lives were lost due to long-standing social pandemics. Additional fears from them brought extra stresses and trauma to many who constantly witnessed it on our many devices.

A pandemic is a widespread occurrence over a whole country or the world at a particular time. Long-standing pandemics existed around the world for centuries that impacted people, hence they are social. Social pandemics impacting people world-wide that are discussed here include racial and health injustices, income inequalities, harsher weather conditions due to climate change because of human activities and threats to democracy.

These social pandemics occur worldwide due to the decisions of people. Some people are taking big risks today without clear thinking as they seek to go back to harsher times. Many people want to make sense of this period as they seek to bring back what was normal from the past, and some people want to establish more positive new normals to improve life for more people.

Something a Little Different.... You may find that Dr. Mapp's books connect information from perspectives that differ from the status quo, or how people "normally" deal with existing social issues. Her family experiences over generations displayed courage, resilience and determination in doing things differently. Her civil rights activist parents started her on the road to learn social justice change agent skills that she used throughout her career. This was coupled with formal studies in social studies (B.A.), school counseling (M.A.) with doctoral research in administration and instruction with educational leadership and an emphasis on social justice (EdD).

All these came together with dialectics studies in a person who understood the importance of building positive relationships as the next stage of desegregation in the civil rights era. Throughout her career she helped students, their parents, colleagues and community organizations she volunteered with to change opinions, when needed, to improve their performances.

Dr. Mapp understood early that living, learning, schooling and our families are linked and impacted by historical, political, educational and social forces. This requires a holistic approach for solutions to complex situations for better outcomes. It also requires people to talk about things not normally discussed, including updated attitudes, information and understanding needed for knowledge. Skills to understand a futures orientation are also needed to prepare children for their future lives. This means that schooling and other institutions need to improve, while at the same time we need to protect the Earth, the only place where human beings can live.

In the twenty-first century, changes are needed to improve the lives and performances of individuals, organizations and our environment which supports us. When talking about the future, technology needs to be seen as a tool, not the whole focus. A futures orientation begins with viewing present consequences that were started with past practices. We are not held accountable for what happened in the past, but we do have a responsibility to correct things for our children's futures.

Dr. Mapp's *S.A.U.C.E.* framework is designed to help families and other clients work through today's interconnected areas of information, skills and attitudes for improved outcomes. It helps them *Speak* and eventually *Act* on usually *Unspoken* topics using information and understanding which becomes knowledge. Her questioning and guidance help elicit *Connections.* A positive attitude is also needed to help clients more easily *Embrace* needed changes.

This Framework was developed to support parents and families in empowering themselves to shift home-life while also improving outside influences that impact family life, like schools. By intentionally embedding strategies of well-being and learning into home-life, families can improve what they do at home as the first teachers for their children. Children will then be better prepared for formal education. Then schools can help continue to prepare children for the future world they will inherit. This framework can also help parents and families fill some personal learning gaps which can help them improve their financial security. It is also used with other clients in community groups to shift organizational culture.

The *S.A.U.C.E.* framework's holistic approach recognizes that everything is connected, and that improving outcomes requires a deep understanding of the various factors that come into play. The framework is a powerful tool for empowering families, educators, and communities to disrupt negative patterns and work together towards positive change. Ultimately, the *S.A.U.C.E.* framework offers a pathway for holistic learning that integrates all aspects of individual and collective well-being.

What are your thoughts about this Introduction?
Did the information help you gain useful knowledge?
Was your attitude open or closed to its ideas?
Are you confident of the skills you already have?
Jot down what you want to learn more about or circle areas of interest.

Part 1: What's Needed to Make Sense?

Making sense is needed as decisions are made to move beyond the status quo, or where we are right now. To improve life, we need to get beyond confusion and disarray so our reactions to stressors need to become more positive and proactive. We need to connect what we do on different levels, from the personal, to family, work, community, nation and the world.

> *When we fail to make sense of the past,*
> *we are often trapped in it,*
> *retelling old hurts over and over again.*
> *–Tasha Eurich*

The United States is not yet 250 years old as a nation and it is also trying to make sense. We are near the middle of the "terrible two's" of our second century. Just like 2 year-olds, mood swings and difficult behaviors occur. We cling to the past while seeking independence from it. We bounce between reliance on past true, or false, assumptions and a desire for change at times.

> *As the pandemic rages on it gives us a chance to reimagine*
> *the world by tracing history, not forgetting it. --Chime Asonye*

Some of the changes related to the pandemics need to include different ways of doing things that can make life better for humanity while protecting our Earth. Thus, people must take into account how they feel and react towards others, while examining what's normal and what is to come. The normal was not good enough for many, so shifts in people and systems are needed.

Sense is a word with many shades of meaning that include understanding or becoming aware of something. Sense describes reactions of different parts of our bodies to specialized physical abilities to see, smell, hear, touch and taste. It's a verb of perceptions by the senses, such as to discern, feel or observe. It's the ability to understand, react to or recognize something. Sense making is the process of giving meaning to experience.

Skills, new knowledge and attitude changes are needed to make sense of where we are on different levels. Making sense makes it easier to understand life because background information (the past) is worked through and reflected on to see or sense the many connections occurring in the present. Then plans can be made to gain skills for solutions to problems impacting people and earth for the future.

1. Plan to Make Sense

We all had a deep and abiding faith in God
and feared doing nothing more than doing something.
--James R. Mapp

Doing something rather than doing nothing may be where you are right now. Times are changing and some people seem to hit brick walls as they think of only their point of view. This is the time to make personal changes for the good of families, the nation and world by taking the high road to be more positive as sense is made of why we are where we are. The next step is to do something. Goals need to be set with efforts to move towards them. If mistakes are made, we need to just take a deep breath, learn anew, then try again. Shifts become easier when we understand what needs to happen.

Planning entails thinking and feeling. Some people find that when they write their thoughts and feelings down, it's natural to keep a *journal.* A journal is a record of current reactions and is a good tool to write about thoughts, feelings, dreams and frustrations. Keeping a journal can be relaxing and reassuring. When focus is placed on issues that are written down and reviewed, they may be worked out easier. If you already keep a journal, continue writing in it as you go through this book. You may see areas that need to shift as new goals are reached.

As you read through this book, circle or mark activities and tasks
that you may want to perform, journal about or act on now or later.

Sometimes major goals need more planning and structure with formal written *action plans*. An action plan is a simple, yet detailed list of activities and steps needed to accomplish major goals or objectives. They differ from to-do lists or journaling since they focus on achieving major goals without missing important steps. Before starting any change or an action plan, use **SMART:**

> **S**pecific (clearly defined with what, why and how you'll do it).
> **M**easurable (use evidence so you know the goal was met).
> **A**chievable (it's challenging but you can achieve it).
> **R**esults-focused (measure results, not the activities) and
> **T**ime-bound (date or time frame you want to finish the project).

It's best to work on only one major action plan at a time until you get used to the process since they take more work than simple lists.

Plan your actions when you are ready to set goals to change something in your life. It's best to be specific and precise in writing down intentions for meeting those goals. Note that there are no wrong or right ways to make plans. What is a goal you'd like to meet at this time? You can add other goals as you work through this book.

1. For each action, make a list of steps to work on from beginning to end.
2. Note barriers and work around them, then make time to complete each.
3. Keep the action plan close by to record any changes that are needed.
4. Then note in your journal the improvements you made and still may need to make in working with others or on yourself.

As you read through this book, note those areas you are interested in changing. Then develop a plan to do so. While working on the Action Plan, keep it close by to record any changes. Keep an open mind to lessen frustrations and to keep a positive attitude.

> *There are three kinds of people in the world:*
> *those who make things happen,*
> *those who watch things happen,*
> *and those who wonder what happened.*
> *--Unknown.*

> *What kind of people are you at this time?*
> *You may be using this book as you wonder what happened.*
> *As you make sense about this period you may want to develop into*
> *another "kind of people" for the good of your family.*

2. Continuous Learning with Thinking

...In this huge period of transition,
we have to do a lot of thinking...
Every crisis is both ...danger and ...opportunity. ...
Danger because ... of the damage to our lives [and] institutions...
Opportunity ... to become creative ... and a new kind of people...
                              ----Grace Lee Boggs

Continuous learning is needed to help us think about making sense of today. It's the process of learning new skills and knowledge on an ongoing basis. Continuous learning happens in many ways, from self-learning, to taking formal courses, to learning about history, to just keep up with the times. Self-initiative is needed so individuals can continually learn on their own. It can be challenging but courage can be learned. Continuous learning helps us think, but feeling is also part of that process since people are emotional creatures.

Today a lot is heard about how people "feel" in media and in daily life. Some people may think about things without knowing underlying information that can bring clarity to their thoughts. When people spend a lot of time either feeling (awareness of an emotional state or reaction) or thinking (using the mind to produce thought) in isolation or without the full story, they miss out. Saying things without thinking can lead to hurting others' feelings and doing things without feeling can seem cold and heartless.

Direct links exist between thinking and feeling. When brought together, the sensing, knowing and being of feeling and thinking connects people. They may then seek to be better than they've been taught or choose to change how they live as they become empowered. Some people may believe that feelings and emotions are caused by external forces like the words or actions of others like "you made me do that." Thoughts and beliefs happen quickly and automatically and influence feelings and reactions at that moment.

Thinking changes over time as people mature, though when stressed, they may not think about the consequences for their behaviors. Some adults in different stages of development focus more on their feelings, superficial thinking and how they look rather than how their actions impact others around them. This can occur at home, work, in the community, nationally or even globally today.

Some people view media that supports superficial thinking, like "reality" shows and gaming. They may feel that this media display exciting ways of life with extreme and negative behaviors. They may sometimes mimic these extremes in their lives. Or they may search for it in some shows that seem anti-family and anti-humanity at times, with disrespect and dysfunctions displayed as though they are the new normal. Some people may feel that's the way they should be and act, which is more like older adolescents than responsible adults. Through research we now know that adolescence can last until around 35 years of age today, which used to be considered middle age a few decades ago! Yikes!!

> *Feeling and thinking are directly proportional*
> *to each other and inseparable.*
> *--Anuj Somany*

Common sense. Feeling is important when coupled with common sense or intuition. Gut reactions and feelings are intuition, but they can be based on mood and other psychological factors. Relying on feelings and emotions can cause trouble in making sense, so people need to check themselves to determine if emotions and beliefs are getting in the way of common sense.

For common sense to take effect, thinking and looking at the bigger picture are important while taking time to work through thoughts and feelings. When adults are open-minded and curious, feelings can more easily link with thoughts. When common sense and learning are linked with thinking and positive feelings, relationships can be more positive.

Public schools prepared Americans to be good citizens and good factory workers for more than a century. Students were required to sit still, listen and do exactly as they were told. This type of thinking was lower-order, simple, transparent and repetitive until it became a habit. Students were given facts and content and weren't expected to really think. Students who followed the rules were considered obedient. This type of thinking is used in many workplaces or even in many homes today, though deeper thinking is needed.

Lower-order thinking is used in basic reading and writing since it is easier to understand, teach, learn and test. But today's adults and students need higher-order and critical thinking and feeling skills to make sense of today. The need for these skills requires higher order thinking.

Higher-order thinking requires more interactions and it is more complicated than lower-order thinking. When children play, they sometimes use higher order thinking on a daily basis by being creative, taking on leadership roles, planning and working through problems. Yet, another layer of thinking beyond lower and higher order is needed when major decisions are made.

Think critically as an additional layer of thinking to make sense. It is the ability to think clearly and rationally without bias, prejudged opinions and impulse, which may make it hard for people who prefer to hold on to their biases. It is a complex type of thinking that requires creative thinking and problem solving, questioning and effort and can give more than one solution.

> *Whether you think you can or you can't, you're right.*
> -- *Henry Ford*

Critical thinking, like reading, is not natural but learned. Some critical thinking decisions are complex and solutions may not be obvious, so multiple strategies or clues have to be used or applied. Critical thinking is shaped by beliefs and processing skills which help people manage and modify their actions on a daily basis as they complete tasks. Process skills involve observing, sequencing, communicating, measuring, guessing, and predicting.

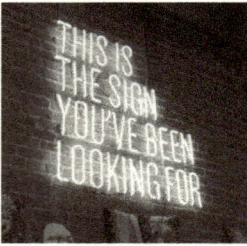

These skills are first learned at home. Sometimes parents teach their children to understand the importance of thinking through tough situations before they happen, which takes critical thinking. Sometimes done in role play before situations occur, this allows them to act more positive, think deeper and be flexible. This may result in better choices while thinking about the consequences.

Decisions are hard for some people to make. A simple way to make them is to make a list of pros and cons. Determine if the pros or the cons are stronger. Then do research or talk to others to see how they resolved similar problems. Make sure that the solutions used are not just opinions but based on research for situations similar to what is being worked on as evidence.

Critical thinking takes work. In order to process and think, people need to be open-minded, curious and strategic. Then they need to think again, making sure to feel where they are in the process. Many people use these skills many times a day and need to know that they are successful in thinking and feeling.

> *The ultimate measure of a man [or woman] is not*
> *where he stands in moments of comfort and convenience, but*
> *where he [or she] stands at times of challenge and controversy.*
> *–Martin Luther King, Jr.*

*We are in a period of challenge and controversy...how do **you** measure up?*

Where wisdom reigns,
there is no conflict between thinking and feeling.--Carl Jung

Use WISDOM Before Making Major Decisions

WISDOM is good judgment leading to sound actions to make sense of things. Try to be calm while figuring out solutions so that wisdom can surface, asking:

Who, what, where, when, why and/or how? Ask these questions to understand situations better or when puzzled and words don't flow easily.

Imagine the future without this disagreement. Was it based on he/she said, emotions, bias or real reasons? Is there supporting evidence?

Stop, think and do what you can to create better times by learning more or use what you already know. Learn more on-line or at the library.

Deactivate stress and share your pain by talking. Think about your loved ones. Let Faith guide you. If it's based in the past, forgive and get over it.

Open your mind and heart to move beyond anger: shift perspectives, forgive the other person, forgive yourself, write it out, let it go and heal!

Motivate yourself and others by being and acting positive. Then ask - is it really that important?

Higher-order Thinking Skills for Deep Learning

HOTS push the brain to learn deeply and do something with facts, not just memorize them. They show connections across subjects and discover truths:

1. Apply: use what is available, what would happen if....
2. Analyze: break into parts, carefully examine; compare and prioritize.
3. Logic: think in rational ways, understand (deduct, induct, abduct).
4. Evaluate: determine its worth, judge the outcome.
5. Critique: consider the benefits and use detailed analysis.
6. Infer: guess or draw conclusions by reading between the lines.
7. Synthesize: combine parts, create, connect, put information together.
8. Reflect: think and make judgments about what has happened.
9. Communicate: share conclusions in various ways.
10. Metacognition: think about how thinking is done.

For Higher-ordered Critical Thinking, Can You:

1. Visualize the problem? Is the information true and credible?
2. Separate relevant information from irrelevant?
3. Seek reasons and causes? Justify solutions?
4. See more than one side of the problem?
5. Use real reasons, not just assumptions?
6. Identify bias (prejudice) or logical inconsistencies?

Is Propaganda Being Used?

Propaganda is a tactic used to manipulate people in everyday conversations, advertisements and politics. The word propaganda is used infrequently in the USA, which is sort of like the use of capitalism. Propaganda is used to make arguments more persuasive, even though they are sometimes untrue. If one of the following scenarios is given to convince decision making, think twice and rely on common sense, research or responsible others to make sense of what is being said:

1. Name calling (tear the opponent down).
2. Get on the bandwagon (they say everybody's doing it).
3. Glittering words (use empty but important sounding words).
4. Testimonial (use a celebrity to endorse it).
5. Card stacking (put things in your favor).
6. Either or fallacy (when the answer is really in-between).
7. Faulty cause and effect (the cause does not bring the result).
8. Appeal to ignorance (seems true but there's no proof to support it)
9. Straw man (exaggerate what's being said so it seems ridiculous).
10. Metacognition (think about how thinking is done or how you think).

Was anything surprising to you in these thinking areas? Why or why not?

Is there an area of extra interest to you that you may want to revisit?

Do you seem stuck where you are?
Answer the questions on the next page to see if they help at all.

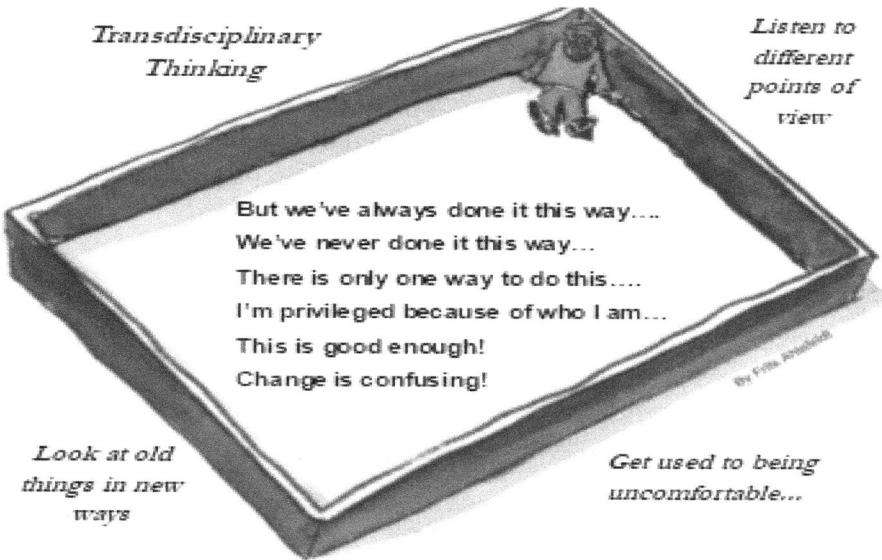

Transdisciplinary
Thinking

Listen to
different
points of
view

But we've always done it this way....
We've never done it this way...
There is only one way to do this....
I'm privileged because of who I am...
This is good enough!
Change is confusing!

by Fritz Afflerbach

Look at old
things in new
ways

Get used to being
uncomfortable...

Are you still IN the box
or
are you working to get OUT of the box? Why?

...attempting to bring about world peace
through the internal transformation of individuals is difficult,
[but] it is the only way. ...
Peace
must first be developed within...
Love, compassion and altruism
are the ...basis for peace
from the individual to family, from the family to the community
and eventually to the whole world.
–Dalai Lama

What do you need to do for peace within yourself?
Are you where you need to be?

3. Literacy in a Democracy

From the very beginning of our Republic,
a well-educated citizenry was thought to be essential
to protect liberty and the general welfare of the people.
Even before the Constitution was established,
Ordinances included responsibilities
of the nation for an education system.
--League of Women Voters

Our education system has always had many problems, but it produced workers needed for each period in our country. Education is one of many national institutions that reproduce inequities in society yet serves the nation's needs.

Literacy is a bridge from misery to hope...
... a tool for daily life... platform for democratization ...
along with education in general, a basic human right....
Literacy is a road to human progress and through which every
man, woman and child can realize his or her full potential.
-- Kofi Annan

Democracy is not perfect, but when comparing it to other political systems, it gives more people choices to improve how they live. We are a representative democracy, but there are other systems, such as direct democracy, rule by experts, rule by a strong leader and military rule. Use this surreal period to improve it though voting has always been restricted in this country.

You can never leave footprints that last
if you are always walking on tiptoe.
--Leymah Gbowee

Strength and courage are especially needed when people's lives feel threatened. During this period of rapid societal changes, jobs and homes have been lost and illness and injuries may have strained budgets with little or no insurance. Things right before the pandemic may have been better for some, but many have multiple jobs making less money with few benefits, expenses keep rising and many are out of work. More working age Americans are dying due to economic stress and lower incomes with two recessions in almost a decade. The global pandemic and racial justice crises cause even more stress.

People have had to get through difficult times that rocked their worlds. They had to make sense of their lives while becoming capable of dealing with setbacks. They had to become more *proficient*, or skilled, in learning how to right things that were wrong. They also had to become more *literate* or educated in knowing how to deal with issues on many levels. Proficiency is not the highest level of learning but the skills to be successful are known.

Literacy is a collection of shared cultural and communication practices that change as society and technology change. People have always had to adjust to what was happening in their communities and society in general to be literate. Literacy helps people make sense of the world. Today, being literate requires a shift in thinking from the simple and clear cut literacy of the past which used to mean knowledge of the *3 R's* of **R**eading, w**R**iting and a**R**ithmetic. With rapid societal and technological changes and competition from other countries, proficiency in literacy has changed to include other skills and attitudes. When considered critical, extra thought is given to benefits and faults of something.

> *Critical literacy is vital in the twenty-first century.*
> *As citizens in a democracy,*
> *we are responsible for thinking deeply about the texts we read*
> *and for interrogating our assumptions and …perspectives…*
> *In short, citizenship requires participation…*
> *based on an understanding that we can question without fear.*
> *--Nancy Frey and Douglas Fisher*

Citizens are legally recognized people who live in a country, but some in the US seem to know little about *responsible civic participation skills.* It's taught in some schools but may not be taught well or sometimes taught by the weakest teachers. Student assessments showed a recent decline in civic understandings. It's interesting that some naturalized citizens and some immigrants might possibly know more about our country and civic participation than some citizens since they had to pass a citizenship test.

Civic engagement is low. Brookings research notes that only 1 in 4 know how our democratic government works and a 2019 study noted that only 17% trust that our national leaders will do the right thing. Citizen participation in community organizations, religious organizations, unions and elections were prevalent during the 20th century but it's now declining.

Media is polarized today and some people don't listen to or trust the news. Some social media leisure pursuits keep discussions about civic problems low in "civic deserts." These deserts impact 60% of all rural youth and 30% of those living in urban and suburban areas. Our actions prove that we don't know enough about being a citizen. New forms of community civic networks are needed. Schools are one of the few social institutions located in every community across the nation that can possibly change the lack of civic engagement. They supposedly have been doing that all along – but not well.

Civic engagement after the viral pandemic will be interesting!
We're almost "after" now. Is the seeming lack of morals, lack of caring
enough to keep profanity at a minimum, lack of caring about helping others
other than just yourself, and lack of knowing how to act with each other part
of this? What are you willing to do to help our nation? Or stay the same?

Citizenship skills are now being tested in some states so young people have to know more   about how to participate in and support our democracy, which is government by the people. What will happen to engage adults?   One civic duty is the completion of the *census,* so the government knows more about its inhabitants and their needs. Hopefully you completed Census 2020 while the pandemic raged since the results last for ten years! Census data helps our nation know the needs of all peoples in each part of the country.

Citizens should be capable of safeguarding our democracy while taking care of its democratic values like liberty, equality and justice. But some don't know that democratic values should apply to us all. Knowing about citizenship helps people make sense of the political process, but first they have to be educated or literate concerning a lot of things. Adults first learned to be literate when they were children at home since parents and families are their first teachers. Schools continue that process, but more is needed in this global 21st century world to be *LITERATE* so:

Learn continually and continuously throughout life; be willing to change.
Interest families and youth in being active to improve their communities.
Think critically to make wiser decisions to gain better solutions to problems.
Evaluate situations before acting, look for connections and be flexible.
Remember that everything is connected, check attitudes to pursue peace.
Apply what's learned at home to school, life, careers and our democracy.
Take time to learn innovation skills to be capable, creative and literate.
Engage and share in cultural literacy to better communicate with diversity.

Be literate by working to be proficient with at least *adequate* understandings of many things like our democracy and understanding ourselves. Skills needed to learn more about our nation and ourselves can be challenging at times. When skills are challenging, use or apply them through analysis (studying) and investigations (by observing and examining) them. Everyone should be able to improve their literacy skills while helping our democracy improve. When literate, people can react and act on what's going on around them. Sure, they can just criticize, but in a democracy people can act.

2020s Actions Defined. Cancel-culture, anti-woke-ism, futuring and a futures orientation are four ways that people in a democracy have moved beyond complaining to acting. Some of them are speaking and acting on topics that in the past were not talked about in the media, so were unspoken to a degree. They were complaints that people made in their own circles.

But the isolation of the viral pandemic gave people time to really think and plan wide-spread actions related to the social pandemics that became in-your-face topics of discussion on all our devices. Social media acted as an equalizer so people could express anger and outrage. The nature of social media makes responses grow quickly as data is quickly added. The recent onslaught of the long-standing social pandemics brought harsh realities to the surface. They were not viewed by just our nation, but the whole world which also had its own problems in the same areas.

The first widespread actions were reactions to wrong-doing when celebrities and leaders acted unethically on different occasions when they were held accountable for abusing power. #MeToo was an accountability movement that was more positive to victims. Few ways existed to voice opinions on topics like these, but a few trending groups on Twitter found a way.

People who were historically marginalized (i.e., Black people) were in the forefront of the first waves of these actions. Later cancel culture perpetrators on the left, right and in the anti-woke movement are sometimes rich, privileged and powerful elected officials and corporations. The early groups used that forum to vocally dictate wrong-doing, spread the word and quickly jump to conclusions. These actions got others thinking about the need for change. That media was used to *cancel-culture* or socially censure or shame people and businesses by withdrawing or cancelling support for them or getting them fired.

But negative things can happen when social media strikes out quickly whether by left or right leaning groups. Doxing happens who private or identifying information is published with the intent to harm. Sometimes people standing up for those who were cancelled were turned on or were dragged through a tough time because they said something that the online "mob" didn't like –

even over minor differences. Some young people looking for validation from peer groups may be impacted if they think differently so they go with the crowd rather than express different opinions which is not healthy for the individual nor for our democracy. This can create loneliness, fear and increase mental health problems.

Some people on the far right and far left think that political correctness, or being careful to use language or behavior that does not offend others, is a problem. They are working to dismantle civil rights to make themselves un-woke and politically correct about European Americans rather than its original intent. Historically "woke" has been around for almost a century so people are alert to racial prejudice and discrimination which hurts our nation and its people.

Today's anti-woke sentiments attack cancel culture, diversity and political correctness that made things a little better for BIPOC (Black, Indigenous Peoples and Others of Color) peoples for a while. They also ban books, endorse gerrymandering to make voting harder and other things. Anti-woke is bad for business but also for today's young people who are the largest diverse group in the world. They will have a lot of messes to clean up as they enter their futures.

Another way to react to and act on is that of *futuring*. I heard about this term decades ago from Grace & Jimmy Boggs concerning their activities in planning a more positive future for Detroit. Futuring is an approach to design future scenarios based on current trends, challenges and opportunities. It is based on hope and it can help communities and individuals question assumptions made about life.

Writing and sharing stories techniques are used as next steps to solve problems through discussions and collaboration. It does not predict but looks at the present and raises informed projections with imaginative critical design to think differently about issues. It allows people to step back from fear and proactively design steps to change things for the better. Any age persons can be futurists, but knowledge is needed to envision what might and can happen. Know that you are futuring now.

It's often not a lack of skills that lead to change failing,
but a fundamental lack of understanding of
how others will be affected by change and an
inability to successfully communicate the reasons for change.
In other words, a lack of change literacy.
--Patrick Mayfield

When people are literate, they can change more easily. ***Change literacy*** (Jim Russell) is a management technique that leverages relationships to bring about change. It recognizes that human behavior usually follows predictable patterns. Rather than use silo thinking where one leader becomes the hero, change literacy intentionally uses innovation to include all stakeholders in the process. Reasons for change are explained even though it can be disruptive. The mnemonic **LITERATE** used earlier in this chapter is useful in eliciting change during this surreal period.

The present pandemics caught most people throughout the world unaware, in some ways, but changes from them will be long-lived. We learn what's going on during this period using our senses of hearing, seeing, clearly communicating and feeling using reports and other resources. We think, observe, learn, and communicate. This is what literacy is all about.

Futuring was done before the pandemics and is needed as we work through racial disparities, a huge problem of a nation developed For and By the People. You may have spent time futuring, or thinking about making life better in the future, but possibly without next steps. It is up to each of us to make this period better than the one before since we're dealing with consequences of past actions that need to be rectified. Many human activities are working to destroy our earth and the peoples living here. Money or financial gain drives this and its want has been in the forefront of the actions of many for centuries around the world.

Before moving farther, it's important to present a **futures orientation** for a shared vision that takes into account facts on where we are at this stage, how we got here and what else needs to happen to change the trajectory of our lives. For the future, we need a vision, working together collectively, resilience to bounce back when bad things happen, self-discipline to stick to plans and adjusting from where we are to something better.

To get a clearer vision of today as you envision your future, look at this important 15 minute video that may guide you to the next phase of your life since it is futures-oriented: ***A Future for Us All*** by Sir Ken Robinson at https://www .youtube.com/watch? v=r1v31ZEIins Show and discuss it with your children since it directly impacts their generation. Show it at school for teachers and students to discuss and learn from it. School projects, future careers and even how to remake schools may become outgrowths of its showing.

We're at a tipping point where we need to make changes to heal our earth while healing relationships among so many. Healing from racism means that individuals have to unlearn the racial messages that were internalized, possibly since childhood and across generations. Healing is needed for those being racist and those receiving racism. The information in this book will be useful to both groups as they heal themselves and society. Since everything is connected, healing relationships can more easily move to us towards healing our earth, too.

Confronting the racist policies
within our society requires us to confront
the complicity, complacency and ignorance
within
ourselves.
-- Tate H. Aldrich

Your family of origin influenced you in many ways.
They were influenced by society's treatment and expectations of them.
What have you learned about your family's many influencers?

Are the same influencers still at work
Or have changes been made to dampen their influence?

Part II: The Personal Becomes Political

There's an epidemic going on right now
and it's a lack of courage.
It stems from the inability to hold ourselves accountable...
To avoid accepting responsibility for our decisions,
playing the victim...not honoring who we are...what we believe in.
—Justin Miller

Everyday actions are personal and private, but when shared through stories, people may find that others like them share those same life experiences. The personal then becomes public when people become conscious of larger societal and political issues that are connected to their personal lives. These issues become political when power relationships in government are added, but it takes courage to look below the surface. The larger systemic and political issues impact and influence personal issues, and vice versa.

Before going further, it's necessary to look at a term that's not used often today, but it is a part of who we are. We are human beings who are being human as we consciously change. Human being is a category that people gave themselves rather than it being a scientific category. Humans are able to communicate through words, symbols, bodily gestures and facial expressions.

Humans can change and make decisions, with consequences that affect self and others through social practices. Being human is an attitude. Humans talk and act inhuman at times through their actions, especially in the treatment of other humans. When being inhumane, people lack ethical and compassionate attitudes toward others. This keeps people, or humans, from changing so they can work together harmoniously and peacefully to benefit us all.

Instead of internalizing this legacy of change
and developing on it in such a way that it
frees us to enlarge our humanity,
most Americans hold tight to the status quo
and thereby become jailers of one another.
To create change
is the unique capacity of human beings.
–Change Yourself to Change the World

Change is what humans do - even though some resist it. The "personal is political" as a term seemed to come from the feminist and student movements of the late 1960's and 70's era. But these same understandings and actions were used centuries before by colonists against the king of England and the enslaved against those who owned them or treated them as less than human.

Whenever one person stands up and says,
'Wait a minute, this is wrong,'
it helps other people to do the same.
-- Gloria Steinem

CONFIDENCE
WORK
SUCCESS
TEAMWORK
MOTIVATION
INTELLIGENCE
CREATIVITY

Acknowledging the personal as a part of the political arena takes courage. Courage takes a shift in being, or a mind shift to do something to overcome barriers and tackle challenges to make a difference.

With courage comes a commitment, though the fear of risks is still present. People who display courage want the good that can happen to outweigh the bad – but they have to be willing to accept consequences and any repercussions. This brings a peace of mind with thoughts of the positive things that can happen. The following words from the past are being played out during this surreal period of time:

We have a powerful potential in our youth,
and we must have the courage
to change old ideas and practices
so that we may direct their power toward good ends.
—Mary McLeod Bethune

When you do the common things in life
in an uncommon way,
you will command the attention of the world.
—George Washington Carver

4. Personal Stories

Using logic and being mindful
are not the same thing as "trying to make sense."
The former is methodical, it uses a grounded awareness to enact
your true desires, the latter is looking at the product of those
actions and wondering how they got that way.
–Brienna Wiest

This book uses logic and reflection on past experiences to make sense of where individuals are, but also where our country is at this point in time. Generalizations are broad written or spoken statements that are not true all the time. They are used since they are clear cut, one dimensional and easy to defend. Making sense means moving away from generalizations. To move away from generalizations, specific problems need to be identified in specific ways to make sense of them. This requires work since fear, confusion, frustration and a lack of patience can keep people from delving deeper. Some people delve deep all the time because they develop habits in this area.

Making sense begins with understanding connections of the stories or narratives that each of us experienced from our youth. When national historical connections are made with them, a more complete story can surface. When we really see our personal lives clearly with its many complex stories, we can begin to see the complexities of life in general. When we share our stories with others, more of us may be able to move away from simple generalizations.

Life Story Connections. Stories are powerful. They can help build connections and influence people more than just facts and details and they can inspire and educate. The U.S. is at a crossroads in some ways....

Over the past two decades in America,
the enduring, complicated divides of
ideology, geography, party, class, religion, and race
have created deep fractures in the United States,
each side fighting to advance its own
mythology and political interests.—Roger Cohen

What are we today? Can we embrace more positive ideas again? One way to attempt to do so is through story. Think about your life story and jot a few notes down in your journal. This will help you begin to make sense of your past. Think about the positive and negative things that may have shaped you.

Did any crisis become turning points in your life? Also consider early memories or important memories during childhood and adulthood, plus anything else of importance to you. Consider stories passed down in your family.

> *Sometimes your biggest challenges are going to be*
> *you versus you.*
> *—Andy Henriquez*

Then write at least a paragraph about each of the following **CONNECT** points with what happened personally, when and the people involved. Hopefully this exercise will help you become more self-aware as you connect your story to today, which can help you determine your future self.

Chapters of your life are like those in a book. Select remembered events that were important to you. What were you and others thinking and feeling?

Over time, changes happened. What do events say about who you are today?

Notice any major themes, feelings or lessons learned from your story. Did you notice any contradictions or misconceptions you had about anything?

Notice things about the kind of person you are and who you may want to be.

Expectations and reactions may have popped up those impacted others. Read your story, then determine what it might be saying about your values, passions and patterns. How and why did events happen with results?

Complexities may be evident in your story with different perspectives, many explanations and contradictions. Is it clear cut and simple or messy?

Themes may have run throughout your story through what you felt or thought. What were they? Do you want to use them to make changes?

Hopefully you have started journaling your story by now. Before writing, it's best to figure out what's problematic and what's not. Are there family secrets that seemed to not notice that problem areas existed? Think about them. When trying to move ahead, you have to first be able to *admit that problems exist* that need correcting. Problems of others abound, but personal problems have to be faced too.

Questions are being faced around the world and we can no longer hide from contradictions on different levels. Populations move today because of past problems. People have become more negative all around the world. Hate and contradictions have become more popular by more people, it seems. Until people can admit that problems exist, they are in denial and problems will continue, especially when surrounded by people with the same viewpoints.

When problems are admitted, it takes time to prepare for new ways of doing things.

When the journal, action plans and information from this book are brought together, they can serve as clues to piece together how you might react in the future. Using the clues in this book, individuals can choose to build or renew relationships, wellness and well-being as they consider living more healthily and peacefully by themselves and with others. Well-being is being well-balanced, happy, prosperous and/or successful. Wellness occurs when actively doing things to become aware of and make choices to be healthy and fulfilled. It's all up to you as an individual with free will.

You may even go through a paradigm shift as usual ways of thinking and doing are replaced by changes in approaches or underlying assumptions. You begin to see things differently when your paradigm shifts. This is part of the continuous learning that's needed by all during these fast-paced and troubling times. Together these may result in deeper and wiser understandings of connections, courage and commitment to change. You may even find civic awakenings, more enjoyment of relationships, work or more positive changes. The two pandemics are affecting a lot of people nationally and globally.

> *The coronavirus pandemic*
> *is going to cause immense pain and suffering.*
> *but it will force us to reconsider*
> *who we are and what we value,*
> *And, in the long run,*
> *it could help us rediscover*
> *the better version of ourselves.*
> *--Politico.com/new... 21 March 2020*

We may reconsider who we are as we work on personal stories. At times emotions from the past may surface, especially if existing life events were threatening or negative in any way. To get through emotions, use the **RAIN** approach (Firestone and McAdams, 2019): **R** for recognize, **A** to accept, **I** to investigate and **N** to not be defined by difficult thoughts or events. This activity will create more inner security to help build more positive relationships. Try it on a small problem you are facing in your story.

Continue this process while making responses deeper with the following additions. Record answers to the following questions in your journal or begin one to keep all exercises from this book in one place. Generalizations may seem simple and clear cut to individuals, but others have different points of view. To clear things up, answer these questions:

1. What are you trying to make sense of that you decided to face - your family situation, relationships, your health, job or how you feel about protecting others and yourself or racial justice? Are they personal thoughts or actions that get in the way of formerly good relationships?

2. What do you want to move forward to or move toward, and why?

3. Look at the history of what you're concerned about, whether it's about you, relationships or things outside the home. Research the time period and decade. How did it play out in your community and the nation? What were the similarities or differences with others' lives?

4. Is the problem still here? What are you willing to give up or negotiate?

Answers to these questions can lead to ***personal growth with empowerment***. It includes self-development or self-improvement towards transformation (a dramatic change). It involves growth of all parts of a person. This includes feelings about themselves and how effective they feel in their lives. This can be tied to education and continuous learning since learning more is part of the human need to improve. It can even become a paradigm shift!

Brain research has proven that problems and pains in real time today are interpreted from lessons from earlier lives. Our brains are like data processers that create, store and allow access to information. Talking about or even writing down stories can start meaningful change within and can help with healing from harsh events. This has implications for our society, also, since personal narratives or stories are connected to national narratives.

As a collective of peoples in these United States, Americans need to see the complexities of our national lives so we can move away from simple generalities espoused by too many people that are not true. This book will help readers to hopefully see and understand the complex nature of our history that was neither clear cut nor simple. Our nation's history was filled with myths that made good stories. When we can make better sense of our lives, we can grow to be those Americans whose documents, though not actions, were considered good for the world.

In every culture and every religion,
stories have played critical roles
in constituting meaning,
constructing identity and
prescribing behavior.
--Godsil and Goodale, America Healing

Take a minute to look at the picture on the next page. Is it a duck or a rabbit? It's a reversible figure that's hard to see both figures at the same time. When some see both, they may be amazed for a moment. Think about this picture as you think about other events in your life. When perceptions change, awareness comes.   What you see can dictate how you think.

Our perceptions are like that as we try to make sense of our world. We have to admit that many opinions exist and have to be taken into account to see a more complete picture or story of the "truth." In this global world that can grow more unstable in a few seconds due to technology, we have to begin to see our world through a lens that's not black or white, not true or false, but grey.

Life is never black or white.
It's always in the shades of grey.
Black or white is an easy label
but living life in the grey areas pushes you further.
There is much more to explore in the realm of uncertainty
than there ever is in the realm of certainty.
–Donnalynn Civello

Diverse opinions count from different people, and we have to learn how to work more peacefully together within this new context. None of us are perfect, and we all need to recognize our own shortcomings as the same questions are struggled with through different ways of approaching and answering them. Others may not agree to the various ways we understand, but people need each other. We may have to agree to disagree, but it's hoped that the other side's opinions can matter. It's not just about you.

Life is filled with complexities and possible contradictions that are connected to how we live our lives. Our lives begin with our families and how we were raised or reared in communities that supported or undermined our futures. The next big event in life is education, which continues the learning started by your families as your first teachers.

Some of the following information may be useful for adding more information to the narrative story in your journal..   Answer the following questions while thinking about your past or present family. Use the acronym of **PEACE** since everybody, and especially our families with children today, need peace:

Parenting styles – were your parents strict, permissive, neglectful, flexible?
Expectations - do you or did your parents expect a lot or a little from you?
Aspirations- did parents support your dreams & hopes? Did you feel loved?
Confidence/certainty-did you believe you could learn and they helped you?
Effective home rules that had to be followed. Did you rebel? Why?

Yes/ No or Maybe So?!?
Did you get the benefits you expected to get from your parents/families?

Was your family unavailable because they were dealing with tough issues?

Is it time for you to break any multigenerational situations that became problems in and for your family? Do you need to learn the whole story? Ask!

Colorful demonstrations and weekend marches are vital
but alone are not powerful enough to stop wars.
Wars will be stopped only when soldiers refuse to fight,
when workers refuse to load weapons onto ships and aircraft,
when people boycott the economic outposts of Empire
that are strung across the globe.-
-Arundhati Roy, Public Power in...Empire

It all begins with individual choices!!!!

5. The U.S. FAMILY from Past to Present

History is a story not only of the past, but of the future.
--Grace Lee Boggs, age 100

For most of human history, family relationships were taken for granted. People were born into a particular place at a particular time, into a set of relationships with well-defined responsibilities. They knew what to expect of others and others knew what to expect of them. No matter how, why or when peoples arrived here, they all had to adjust. New families were created, and new patterns of living were developed without past patterns and rules. The best, worst and in-between patterns for living were bequeathed to the future in ideals at our nation's beginnings that still haven't been met.

As time passed, people made decisions to make the best of new situations and isolated conditions, leaving some political struggles to politicians. They strived for the right to be free of cruelty and past inequities, while inflicting it on others. Lives were based on creativity, self-reliance, discipline, community, commerce, initiative and future hope. Nobody made it alone.

Many contradictions exist in this land of freedom, where too many have to fight for the right to life, liberty and the pursuit of happiness. Since World War II families struggled and sacrificed to give their children more material goods while moving to a consumer society and more economic self-interests which fed capitalism. Seeing themselves as victims, they sought scapegoats.

Ideals (perfect examples) in families and our nation have shifted during the last 60 years and many more American children and families are in crisis. We placed money before people. Many families have too much or too little of some things, not enough well-being and wellness and children suffer.

Love, caring and peace are needed to protect our nation from itself. Also needed are faith, hope, courage and lessons learned from the past while building a better future for all of us, no matter when we arrived. We are basically unhappy, with stressful lives and only some of us have liberty.

Youth are gaining more power because of technology, new skills and open eyes, but some are losing hope. Some youth are demanding that they be taught to be capable of working towards the best of solutions to complex problems during, seemingly, the worst of times for some families, our nation and world.

Ordinary people can do extraordinary things.
---President Barack Obama

How does your family's story fit into this rendition of our national history?

We can still alter our course. It is not too late.
We still have options.
We need the courage to change our values
to the regeneration of our families, the life that surrounds us.
--Chief Oren Lyons

Family history is important. You grew up in a family that went through good and bad times and they changed over time. They can't go back to a better time because each time had its own problems and benefits. At one point, people thought that living in certain areas kept families insulated from what were considered as urban, big city problems. But these same problems now occur in small rural communities and rich private suburban enclaves. Money insulates a little and some things were hidden in the past, but nowadays more is coming out related to ethical decisions and cancel culture.

Complex problems seen today can sometimes defy the imagination. We treat "other" people with little dignity and respect at times and feel that brandishing weapons in public is okay – by some people. Too many children don't know both parents, even their brothers and sisters, live in chaotic circumstances and some have little hope. We usurp laws that protect the Earth and seem to want hate to overcome being polite. Today some may even wonder what news is truth or lies.

Check out the *Family Pledge for Peace or Non-Violence*.
If you agree with it,
try to use it in your home every month for a year to change habits. Start soon!

Some people may think their family went the "wrong way" or feel clueless as they work to make a difference in their lives. But don't despair. Some might call clues theories and some old wife's tales, but many variables are involved. Individuals and families are different with their own perspectives or ways of doing things.

Each action taken by any person as they go through day-to-day life is like a puzzle - with some pieces that fit and some that don't. Be positive and act in moderation, persevere and be resilient, bending like trees in the wind when bad things happen, but bouncing back! Be resilient!

To act in a world whose problems seem overwhelming
requires being able to use the powers of
critical and creative thinking
and compassionate and inclusive care.

Employing these tools, adults and youth alike
can act effectively and conscientiously
to solve problems big and small, global and local.
—*S. G. Cannon*

An *influence* is the power to be a compelling or important force that can produce different effects on the actions, behaviors or opinions of people. Certain things influence, but don't predict outcomes that happen in life. An influencer is a person with the power to affect purchase decisions or sway target audiences since they have specialized insight into specific subjects. Some young consumers are starting to turn away from paid influencers for grassroots communities where authentic like-minded peers offer reviews. But we have to be careful that we follow people for real reasons, not just popular.

Choices and decisions begin with individuals since humans have agency or the free will to act independently to make choices. Just think about when you were growing up, your parents told you what to do but you chose to do what you wanted. But on the other hand, you were sometimes influenced by others who swayed you to do "it." Some influencers are directly connected to systemic problems and need to be analyzed and changed for the good of all. Influencers impact systemic racism, poverty and environmental racism. Many times, we agree with them just because – without thinking or checking the research.

Connections need to be made among systemic racism, poverty and the environment where people live. The effects of influencers cut across national and family decisions and we sometimes wonder why we support certain causes without looking at who the influencers really are. Sometimes we just agree without really thinking things through or doing the research so we're sure. Think about the following. Some may wonder why immigrant children in the US are illegally separated from parents, or why more Black children are poorer or why so many children are homeless today, or why so many children are still undereducated.

 It's an American societal thing: in addition to owning children and families for centuries, we are the only United Nations member country that never ratified the most comprehensive human rights treaty on children's rights. In our country over the last two decades, the United Nations in a 2017 report noted, extreme poverty has grown. They reported more homelessness, unsafe sanitation and sewage disposal practices and police surveillance, criminalization and harassment of the poor. Is this why leaders wanted to leave the United Nations? A former President would not allow Jewish children to enter the US to save their lives during the Jewish holocaust. Holocaust is defined as destruction or slaughter on a mass scale, especially caused by fire.

Check out one of many examples of the American rendition of holocaust in US Red Summers from 1919 - 1923.

Influencers usually expect that they can sway people to forget who they really represent and accept what they say, just because. At times, influencers are a form of propaganda, as in celebrities who are paid to support a certain cause but don't. People trust them just because.

The Source of Black Poverty Isn't Black Culture, It's American Culture: Americans don't want to imagine that our racist history is actually an ongoing, racist reality. —Philip Bump

Culture can influence families and shape how people communicate, view conflict and define, solve and resolve problems. Culture is a set of patterns that integrate human behavior around activities within a social group or community. Cultural elements include people's customs, beliefs, actions and values, laws, language, social standards, religious beliefs and traditions, etc.

Families have cultures, but businesses and other entities also have their own cultures or the ways they behave. Cultural identity is the feeling of belonging to a group. People belong to many cultures and become culturally competent when they understand how culture shapes people's beliefs, values and ways of being. Cultural responsiveness means that people pay attention to other's cultural views respectfully. They tolerate, listen and try to understand.

Culture and racial identity. Family culture and racial identity are important to all races, not just to those of color. Racial identity includes a person's view of self in reference to other races. Your self-acceptance, confidence and self-awareness are sometimes connected to how your parents and family members dealt with and judged differences among people, media   images and any segregated home and community environments. These are learned experiences that can be overcome by introducing healthy racial identity from children to adults so it becomes a natural part of living.

Family composition is important and influences children's development, academic achievement and their adult choices. Other issues around families that impact adults are sensitive issues that are private. Your story and life may be related to the composition of your family of origin or family who you grew up in. Children with only one parent involved in their lives can suffer, some more than others. They are more likely to live in poverty, develop behavioral problems and are more exposed to abuse, especially from live-in friends of the single parent. Many girls who grow up without a father grow up too quickly.

Boys may show antisocial behavior to hide the fact that they want and need a father or father-figure in their lives. When children grow up with a mother who may be absent physically or emotionally, they can suffer long term damage to self-esteem, guilt for thinking they're the reason for the mother's leaving, trust issues with other adults, trouble building relationships and possibly a lifetime of grieving can occur. All children need both parents in their lives, so choose wisely before becoming intimate with someone!

> *I came to understand the role of trauma*
> *caused by parental abuse, neglect, and abandonment*
> *and how these traumas*
> *then affect the developing brain and the mind.--Natasha Khazanov*

When both parents are present, but uninvolved or neglectful, problems also occur. These parents are consumed with their own needs and neglect to rear or raise their children. They may allow children a lot of freedom, be friends rather than parents, have few rules and/or they don't provide structure for healthy emotional development. They shift most responsibilities on to older children, relatives or assume that organizations will take care of their children.

Their children can be lonely with little love and social skills, and they are apt to be emotionally, physically and emotionally disconnected from people. They can also have academic and behavioral problems. This may make it hard to find and keep jobs and they may have legal troubles because of their choices. When children are involved too early in sexual matters they are placed at risk. They can experience psychological problems and more abuse with antisocial activity like drug use and more sexual activity. These behaviors can impact learning with academic problems with little hope and interest in the future. The media and lax family situations can influence this involvement. .

Trauma is a disturbing or deeply distressing experience that is emotional and psychological. It can overcome a person's ability to cope, diminishes how they see themselves, causes feelings of helplessness and can keep them from feeling. If trauma is not processed, emotions can become stuck until healed.

Do you know anyone who has been traumatized?

Were attempts made to heal or was the trauma overlooked?

6. The Personal Impacts the Political

As we encounter each other, we see our diversity —
of background, race, ethnicity, belief –
and how we handle that diversity
will have much to say about whether we will in the end
be able to rise successfully to the great challenges we face.
                                                    ---Dan Smith

Each individual has a personal side as a human being, but the personal is influenced by the political in many ways. The public and political come into the personal arena due to the power of laws and policies. They regulate and impact what individuals can do and what we do individually can impact forces in power, to a degree. This is played out repeatedly all over the world at the same time. Peoples are presently in great challenges that involve the personal, the political and our Earth. These connections need to be seen together since they depend on each other to continue existing.

As humans we share many common traits, but we are also different. Diversity is variety or difference. Historically the US has been the most internationally and religiously diverse country in the world and we still are today. Most people came here as immigrants and were given certain benefits if considered the "right" ones. Other groups with a different history:
1. Native/Indian Americans who peopled the Americas and didn't need discovering. (US leaders followed examples of the Iroquois Confederacy Great League of Peace as a part of our representative democracy).
2. Africans who were enslaved and brought here as property for free labor and considered by Claud Anderson as Native Black Americans.
3. Mexicans who were annexed with their land.

The history of each wave of Americans had different stories which can inform the narrative of your personal story. To learn more, read Takaki and Stefoff (2008) *A Different Mirror: A History of Multicultural America.* It's available in free online pdf chapter excerpts and there's a children's version. View *Amend: The Fight for America* docuseries hosted by Will Smith (2021).

Diversity. People are different or diverse from each other, individually and in groups. Families in the same community differ from each other and individuals within families differ too. This is due to factors or traits they're born with (biological) and things in their surroundings (environmental). Biological features of diversity include age, ethnicity, race, gender and physical and mental abilities. Ethnic groups share common or distinct ancestry and cultural practices, whereas race is seen or perceived as groups that share distinctive physical traits. Environmental features help shape families and individuals within them because of their experiences. They include education, family status, culture or way of life, communication style, religion, first language, birth order, income, work experience, military experience and geographic locations. These differences impact society and politics in differing ways and vice versa as layers of socioeconomics.

Though separate, these features of diversity are connected to other larger issues and to each other. As we work through changes in our nation, Isabel Wilkerson noted that a new language needs to evolve to move beyond just race or ethnicity to hierarchal relationships, like caste, since they definitely exist. Read about it for something else to ponder about national relationships.

Like the Elephant in the Room...

When people don't talk about issues like eliminating poverty, racism, white supremacy and climate change, the issues still linger in the room like an

elephant. Imagine an elephant in your room right now – it's huge and in your face and nose. The effects of not talking about these biologic and environmental features linger and need to be dealt with so discomforts can heal.

Then positive and honest relationships can be built and motivations for change may grow. Huge feelings about these topics exist and many prefer that things remain the same, but the same old same old is changing. Today, many seemingly rational people are so threatened by the uncertainties around changes in our environment, our health and relationships, that they ignore needed changes. They believe that science is an opinion, rather than evidence gained from trials and studies that give only one part of a solution.

...new discoveries in psychology and neuroscience
has further demonstrated how our preexisting beliefs,
far more than any new facts,
can skew our thoughts and even color what we consider our most
dispassionate and logical conclusions. ...
We push threatening information away;
we pull friendly information close.
Chris Mooney, Mother Jones

Some people feel extra threatened during this period and continue to act harshly around perceived and real differences. They are being examined outright on negative actions related to race or political parties. This could be due to possible guilt or just not wanting to delve into the truth about their actions and our nation. They prefer to stick to untrue generalizations that make them feel safe (until they really think about it). For example, even with the pandemic raging in this nation and the world, fears and lack of thinking keep some of us from making rational decisions. This is like putting your head in the sand, hoping that unseen problems will just disappear!

Race as a biologic feature. We now know that race is a socially constructed concept that is not based on science, but on what people think about others. It usually includes a racial hierarchy from superior to inferior (sort of like caste). Some people may look like a certain race but may not consider that they are that race. Today, people sometimes choose to define their own race or even gender.

> *Race is no[t]… dependent on skin color…*
> *Race does not need biology.*
> *Race only requires … guys with big guns looking for a reason.*
> *--Ta-Nehisi Coates*

Some people feel we should have moved beyond racial issues - possibly to keep from acknowledging race (invisible) at all!? When data is reviewed, *race is still a factor* as recently seen in Black Lives Matter demonstrations and on our many electronic screens. Race is hard for most Americans to talk about due to societal reasons and internal barriers, but racism needs to be disrupted. Some people try to be "polite" and think that if they see other people's skin color, it means bias. But if you don't see skin color, it's as though others are invisible and not counted - which is not good either.

An "ism" is a distinctive practice or system that some may consider the normal way things work. Racism is a major ism in our nation, but it's existed for a long time. It influenced people's demonstration of hate and misunderstandings through war, slavery, the start of nations and laws, etc. Racism happens when legal authority is linked with a powerful group's bias about race, difference and superiority. Racism is carried out in many ways and does not have to include violent and intimidating actions.

Racism is attitudinal and can involve simple jokes and calling people names. It is demonstrated through prejudice (prejudged opinions where people are judged before meeting or learning about them), discrimination, bullying, unfair practices, zero level policies used against differences, etc. Racism impacts other systems since it is at the core of life in the US. Racism is even considered a health issue because of its health inequities. It's an education issue since too many students are discriminated against as education gets them prepared for societal expectations to stay in their lane. Unfair treatment, threats and harassment occur in many facets of life as results of discrimination and racism.

Racism is not in-borne, it is taught at home by many families who sometimes don't consciously do so. We now know that it's best to respect others - no matter how you were raised or taught. We are all racial and cultural beings with identities that vary according to where we stand at a certain time. Yet negative patterns can be changed if choices are made to do so.

Though infrequently mentioned, racism occurs to uphold white supremacy or the belief in the superiority and dominance of European whites. Understanding whiteness is important in eliminating racism. Whiteness is a social construction and is a study of the structures that produce white privilege. Privilege (just because of who you are, you have an advantage over others or certain rights) needs to be acknowledged. When people are aware of privilege, they may be more compassionate and understanding of others. Whiteness and racism are so normal that many don't recognize them.

> *Having white privilege and recognizing it is not racist.*
> *But white privilege exists*
> *because of historic enduring racism & biases.*
> *Therefore, defining white privilege also requires*
> *finding working definitions of racism and bias. ...*
> *Basically, racial bias is a belief.*
> *Racism is what happens when that belief translates into action.*
> *---Cory Collins*

Poverty as an environmental feature. Many environmental features are impacted by income levels due to poverty which is measured by the US Census Bureau. Poverty cuts across biologic and environmental factors of diversity and can be multigenerational. Families who are poor are trapped with either limited or no resources and they are sometimes not well educated.

The US tried a war on poverty with little results other than jobs for professionals and more false assumptions about impoverished people. Many believe they are lazy and unmotivated and can't be trusted to make good decisions about money but they can be taught.. Many in poverty have food and housing insecurities and poor health with limited access to medical care.

Eliminating poverty is especially needed now since more middle-class families are slipping into poverty. Poverty is bad enough as children and their families live with it, but when poor children grow up to be adults, they can have lingering physical and psychological problems. Problems of helplessness due to family turmoil and substandard housing and health issues related to chronic physical stress can happen. Hunger and malnutrition occur on different levels, with limited access to a good education and basic services. Social discrimination and exclusion from community decision making can also occur. Even if families do everything that's needed, getting out of poverty is hard but it can happen.

It's not true you can't do anything about poverty. ...
the political will, and are people willing to reframe the problem,
instead of blaming the person ...
This is a societal issue,
and if we decide to reallocate resources like we did with the elderly
and Social Security...--Gary Evans

Connections exist among all US systems which makes it even harder for impoverished children and families. But it doesn't stop with them, many issues that need to be dealt with in our nation impact all families no matter their incomes. They keep our nation under-developed, so humanity suffers. The following issues impact many:

... Job insecurity and low wages, lack of paid family leave,
childcare that is both poor quality and unaffordable, racial stigma,
and ...trauma of adverse child experiences and racial exclusion...
But it's not only our children who are at risk.
Our current policies are under-developing America.
https://www.raisingofamerica.org/about-documentary-series

Food and wellness. Another systemic problem that is under-developing all of America is our food system (Goel, Nischan, Frist and Colicchio, 2 August 2020, CNN Opinion). US health and wellness are poor for such a rich nation and it's been happening for centuries. Three out of four Americans are obese and have many diet-related diseases. We have poor nutrition and poor health. Men are advantaged in many areas of society, but they have the worse health outcomes (Georgetown University's Center for Men's Health Equity). Too many restaurants serve nutrition-poor foods and too many people have food insecurities and live in food "deserts" without grocery stores.

A popular line in many commercials today is – "it's not your fault" – as though victimhood is good. When it comes to our food system, part of the information that has been given out hasn't been the whole truth so it's not everybody's fault. Many have been unwilling victims as their health has suffered, whether going to doctors or not. Misinformation makes money for many local and multinational corporations. When people are woke and knowledgeable about health and nutrition, they use food and drug guidelines as a start to learn better ways to be well through nutrition. When lives are fulfilled, people are satisfied with their quality of life.

It's hard to be satisfied when education levels impact financial security that leads to poverty, and health suffers because of trusting professionals and advertisers as we make life-sustaining decisions around eating. This topic is definitely personal, but it's also political in that policies, laws and rules dictate and influence the food system, laws that regulate food production and how foods are grown. Our food system has been optimized for efficiency but not nutrition.

Our food system is broken with milk and vegetables being thrown away rather than giving them to people who need it. The US only very recently added breastfeeding as being more nutritious than fake milk for infants. Food lobbyists, pharmacies, food conglomerates, large corporations and our stock market determine policies so they can get richer, but this has to change. We can't continue putting money over advancements needed for humanity.

Changes were made because of the viral and racism pandemics. Changes also need to be made with our food system and other systems that impact all of us, but especially impoverished families. Broader implications around food production and distribution need to be considered, from the seeds grown and imbedded with pesticides, to whether they were genetically modified or not, to the killing of necessary bees for pollination, to the soil food is grown in, to the miles of life-threatening sewage in pigsties, to cows and off-methane gases that hurt the air to even chickens grown in huge areas.

Nutrition takes a back seat, especially when doctors push medicines, powerful pain killers and disease yet know little about nutrition, or how it sustains health and prevents disease. We have the freedom to do as we choose, to a degree, from the foods we eat, proximity to large crowds as well as whether masks are worn or not. But systemic healthcare and our food systems are public and political.

This global pandemic is being observed closely from around the world because the richest country in the world is handling the pandemic worse than all the other countries. We only have 4% of the world's population, but 25% of the fatalities from the disease occur here and more cases of the illness than all other countries. No matter how some politicians and medical professionals lie about the numbers, too many people are put at risk and too many are dying – and   it's not over by a long shot.

Our Earth. What happens on earth is biologic and also environmental since it shapes people's experiences and where people live. People have a responsibility to conserve our Earth since it's the only planet that supports life. Our actions disrupt its ecosystems or complex systems and networks that work together. They need to be healthy to clean water, purify air, maintain soil, regulate climate, recycle nutrients and provide us with food.

Unfortunately, some people don't feel that human activity destroys ecosystems. We read about water problems that harm children in Michigan but don't consider that that problem may be in our own communities. We hear about environmental racism where plants with pollutants were intentionally located in low income and African American neighborhoods but feel those were problems years ago. We don't consider that even if they were "cleaned" up, the soil is still there and subdivisions and even schools have been built on the toxic waste that remains.

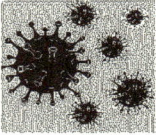

Some people close their ears, minds and hearts to the harm we're causing the Earth, our children and humanity in general. They sometimes don't consider that data learned from science is important. Just think about the allergies and new types of behavior problems impacting children and extreme weather encountered now that weren't as widespread in the past. Deep policy changes are needed that place accountability with personal responsibility. Accountability is a willingness to accept responsibility by checking yourself for your contribution to others' problems. This may be tied to self-work that individuals still need to do. Together the personal and the political are still related!

> *We don't have direct evidence*
> *that climate change*
> *is influencing the spread of COVID-19,*
> *but we do know that climate change alters how we relate*
> *to other species on Earth [which] matters to our health.*
> *Many of the root causes of climate change*
> *also increase the risk of pandemics.*
> *--Aaron Bernstein, Harvard Chan C-CHANGE*

A major connection that is seldom talked about exists among racism, white supremacy and the environment. As we make sense, we have to admit the ties.

> *... [R]acism and white supremacy*
> *harm all of us, ...*
> *in addition to robbing us of our humanity,*
> *racism is also killing the planet*
> *we all share. ...*
> *A long-overdue realization is growing in environmental movement.*
> *It goes something like this:*
> *'We'll never stop climate change*
> *without ending*
> *white supremacy.'*
> *--Hop Hopkins*

> *What do you think about the above symbols of 2020 and beyond?*
> *Where are you at this historic time in history?*
> *Jot some thoughts down and circle areas as you reflect ...*

> *Does the choice I'm about to make or*
> *the action I'm about to take*
> *Heal the future or steal from the future?*
> *-- Francis Litman*

7. The People in Democracy

What we need at the most fundamental level
is a shift in worldview, grounded in a willingness
to see more and exclude less.
Instead, too many of us live in willful denial.
--Tony Schwartz

Democracy is a system of government where citizens exercise power by voting for individuals who supposedly support their viewpoints. Our nation excludes as many people as possible from participating in the simple act of voting in our democracy. This includes prisoners who served their time for felonies, to drawing restrictive voting lines, to people who can't leave work in time, to special pole taxes from the past to picture IDs. Many figure that "they" just don't want to participate by voting, but that's not always the case.

When we begin to get serious about making sense of today, we have to understand national history and how it affected "the people." This area is definitely political because of the power held over people that continues to today. To make sense of history, people have to be awakened and react to what went on in the past and what is really going on in the present. Nothing is as simple as propagandists want people to believe them. Life, democracy and earth are complex and we have to do the right thing for all of humanity.

As a nation, along with the world, we are going through some perplexing times. Sometimes we shake our heads to try to make sense of what is heard or seen on media programming, on-line or even heard in some conversations! Personal and family futures are intertwined with community, national and international uncertainties in real time. Technology gives instant in-your-face information to sometimes unasked questions and world-wide changes.

The triage we see ...
is a result of us never having had a reckoning
with our true history ...
Let's look at what the people who founded this country said
and did because they weren't embarrassed about it.
And that unknown history runs
from 1619 ... to today.
--[Learn about the 1619 Project] --Collier Meyerson

We live amid contradictions where truth and falsities occur at the same time with misconceptions or wrong information about many things. These contradictions and misconceptions are puzzling. They occurred throughout our history and still do within many day-to-day events. Some people are so caught up in not being able to see the truth about history. They live like perpetual Selfies, looking at themselves all the time. They narrow their frame to what's in front of them or to people who think just like them, while losing their way with others.

This reminds me of the story about the ruler who wanted to dress to impress. He was promised an outfit that was invisible to people considered unfit for their positions, unwise or incompetent. In order not to be seen that way, nobody dared say they didn't see the new non-existing outfit. If only selfies were available then! A child uttered the truth that others refused to see. Our country has *dressed to impress* since before its founding in 1776. Bits of history seemed larger than life since our revolutionary ideas changed the world! Ordinary people were talking about the high ideals of self-governance, rather than being subjects of kings and emperors in the feudal system.

We the People of the United States,
in Order to form a more perfect Union,
establish Justice, ensure domestic Tranquility,
provide for the common defence, promote ...general Welfare,
... secure the Blessings of Liberty to ourselves and our Posterity,
do ordain and establish
this Constitution for the United States of America.
—Preamble to the Constitution   https://constitutionus.com/

Our nation began right before the industrial revolution when capitalism was considered as a progressive economic system when compared to feudalism. The size of this country gave unlimited opportunities when the Original People already living here were not factored in. They believed that the land belonged collectively to the People who were to care for Earth.

Our country continues the tradition of dressing to impress with unfair imminent domain at times and the support of policies, multinational companies and board members that abuse the People and our Earth while getting richer – which continues during this pandemic! Feudalism has returned from its medieval counterpart to today's corporate feudalism (Amendment Gazette.com).

... We hold these truths to be self-evident,
that all men [and women] are created equal, ...
they are endowed by their Creator with certain unalienable Rights,
that among these are Life, Liberty and the pursuit of Happiness.
--*The Declaration of Independence*

Future generations were **promised an outfit but it's invisible to the people.** Life, liberty, and the pursuit of happiness were ideals promised to U.S. citizens, and the formerly enslaved thought it was promised to them with Emancipation.   But our government did not develop so that it would be responsible for the good of our society in areas benefiting all the people as they worked to reach those ideals. The outfit that's invisible could be freedom and equality for all the People – while treating all People fairly.

People in the US worked hard to make their lives more comfortable. But contradictions still exist around the owning of people as property and their treatment for centuries afterwards. The enslaved built this country on their backs and many have never been healed from cruelties. Later amendments and laws didn't, and still don't, give too many people justice nor their due. Early settlers who came as immigrants received handouts and "free" land that was stolen from the Native Americans. Even today, some immigrants receive low interest loans while discrimination still exists among Black folk.

The formerly enslaved were promised a mule and 40 acres and received nothing except laws, policies and actions meant to keep them in their places while their owners were paid. When some of them made good lives for themselves despite their treatment they were resented. Whole towns were burned down and lynchings were considered as entertainment for family "picnics."   The effects of these laws and actions are shown even today as people have had to continue to proclaim that Black Lives Matter!

Is this EQUALITY?

If our forefathers and foremothers had done things differently, socially and politically responsible decisions would have been normal in this society. The ideals of balancing power with justice, equality, courage and honesty would have forced us to make different decisions for centuries. We now need to learn more about next steps that need to be taken with the national and international movements for *citizen science* and *ecological economics*. They are part of a transdisciplinary field that aims to improve economic theory and aim to integrate earth's natural systems with human values, health and well-being.

> *WE THE PEOPLE OF COLOR, ...*
> *to fight the destruction ...of our lands... do hereby*
> *re-establish our spiritual interdependence to ...Mother Earth;*
> *to respect and celebrate each of our cultures...*
> *our roles in healing ourselves; to insure environmental justice;*
> *to promote economic alternatives... and, to secure ... liberation...*
> --*Preamble, 17 Principles of Environmental Justice*
> https://www.ewg.org/enviroblog/2007

Well-meaning activists have always had to fight local, state and national governments for amendments and laws. They fought to benefit the people and our Earth for needs like clean air and water, sanitation, safe housing, jobs, justice, fairness, etc.   Actually, in a representative democracy, everyday citizens and people living here should not have to be labeled as activists to carry out important roles as engaged participants in our democracy. Some people seem to want barons from aristocratic societies to keep people in their place, not knowing that their people would probably be subjugated against, too, because of their family ties and lack of money.

People considered unfit, unwise, incompetent - or different. This can be likened to how some people are still treated in our country today. The U.S. has always had diversity or the inclusion of different people within our country. Unfortunately, many interpret differences in our population as bad or inferior, not just as facts, to keep some people down.

Diversity, unity and inclusion could/would/should work together! With diversity comes the handling or mishandling of relationships. Relationships are the ways that two or more people talk to, behave toward and deal with each other.   Relationships are supposedly important to the functioning of a nation developed "for, of and by the people" as unified states developed into one nation. Our democracy, which is government by the people, is suffering because we are not working together as a nation.

Some of us never get the relationship part right because of national and personal contradictions and misconceptions. Relationship problems and educational decisions contradictory to national ideals started early in our nation's history. Many Americans live in denial about important topics like these. Yet these contradictions allow some of us to stay blinded to the use of power, control and privilege that favor one group over others. Power is control over others, and privilege is assumed rights or benefits over others. Our many "isms" like sexism, classism, racism, individualism, etc., seem normal since we try to pretty up our many discriminatory attitudes and behaviors.

Out of the mouths of babes. Our children are trying to inform us about our lives today that border on this story, and some adults are listening. All across the country and world some youth raise their voices as they search for purpose in their lives. Most recently Generation Z climate activist, Greta Thunberg and young millennials, Alicia Garza, Opal Tometi and Patrisse Cullors, who founded the Black Lives Matter movement, have garnered the attention of many around the world. Fortunately, some adolescents protest inequities in society, serve others and try to be their best selves.

While a few try to join the wrong side in foreign wars, join hate groups or gangs, some adolescents inflict hurt on themselves and others – like adults do. We have a lot of work to do to save our children, but we need to save ourselves, too, since we're all in this together. The major problem with our children is that we're not making life better while they're young - while leaving them huge problems that they will need to solve and resolve. Voting is very important, but it's only one thing needed for a democracy to grow. Adults need to improve ourselves to do better for next generations.

Gaps are intentionally left to keep family secrets secret and national secrets away from inquiring minds. Youth's knowledge also includes many gaps in how and why we live a certain way; how and why we need to get along with others different from our families; and why and how we all need to do more than just survive, but need to thrive. Some of us adults don't even know why or know who really did what in our nation's history. We need to do better!

Many play at doing democracy, which is sometimes simply defined as government by the people with rules of the majority winning. Unfortunately, conversations usually don't include how to live in or keep a democracy. We got it by fighting a war, but we don't sustain it or know how to keep it going when we do have it. It's hard to make sense of these times when we don't know enough. Continuous learning, as in using this book, helps.

> ***Democracy needs to be re-born in each generation***
> ***and education is its mid-wife.*** —*John Dewey*

Citizenship or civics was relegated to a sometimes-boring class in fourth grade and/or ninth grade. It may not be taught in some districts now, though some states are testing students on their skills in civic engagement before they graduate. Responsible civic participation supports our democracy but too many citizens prefer to tear down rather than build this important skill.

Civic relates to the duties or activities of a town or city. Civic participation was recently listed as one of the social determinants of health (healthy people 2020.gov). Social determinants of health are environmental conditions that support health. They are represented by place (geography) or where people live, work, school, etc. Civic participation can improve health, economic stability, education, neighborhoods and helps people make sense of social and community contexts. Social relates to society and people are social beings.

To cope with a changing world,
any entity must develop the capacity of shifting & changing–
of developing new skills and attitudes;
in short, the capability of learning. --A De Gues

Though some people zone out, it's best to learn to cope and help improve the changes in our world rather than be victims of change. History and continuous learning, whether through formal education or alone, can help people better understand their personal selves, collective lives and some contradictions as Americans, if different perspectives are allowed. Some people have to read between the lines to cause shifts in how they see the world. Better relationships can be built but it depends on how and sometimes what people learn.

Some people need to know who benefits from certain information about others. They have to struggle to overcome personal bias and prejudged opinions which can make them feel threatened, while they may sometimes threaten others. Most importantly, people need to guard against refusing to believe something just because they wish some contradictions to remain true or false. Some people even refuse to get to know other cultures or family members due to this.

Some people may have started to show dislike for family members from other cultures, though more respect was shown for a period when many in the nation voted overwhelmingly for President Obama. Many wanted to have hope but the racism within our nation kept change from happening. They then chose to vote – or not vote – for someone who wants to tear down our democracy. Too many people support negative acts to feel better about themselves.

Big business is considered by some as people in our capitalistic society. It controls our nation outright with corporate personhood in a system which has really become feudal capitalism. As people learn more from history and changed opinions, they may be able to see and use connections to solve complex issues that are prevalent today. Though the power of corporate and individual greed can try to overtake that – if allowed.

Hopefully with the present crises, we will develop the courage to change from business as usual away from the status quo. People may exclude less when they work to build relationships with others. But first, they have to take time to learn about themselves. This can lead to people doing their best. The pandemics have fast-forwarded change, though some of it is superficial.

Some people are where they need to be at this time, but some are still hurting from past events that impact present behaviors tied to the past. Some people wallow in hateful actions to try to fill better. In order to move from where they are to more success, some people may need to fill in historical blanks with more of the whole truthful story. This can begin the healing process since healing from the past is necessary in many families and individuals. Healing from the past is also needed in our communities and nation.

These pandemics have created multiple crises on many levels, and we are at a turning point in our nation and world. President Barack Obama spoke about the courage needed to work against threats to American democracy and racial justice when he eulogized Rep. John R. Lewis. He spoke about the need for Americans to turn towards each other rather than turning on each other at this time.

Not by sowing
hatred and division,
but by spreading
love and truth.
Not by avoiding our responsibilities
to create
a better America and a better world,
but by embracing those responsibilities
with joy and perseverance
and discovering that in our beloved community,
we
do not
walk alone.
— President Barack Obama in eulogizing Rep. John R. Lewis, civil rights hero

---

Are you more negative or positive?

How did your personal story help or hinder you?

8. Personal Decisions and Our Humanity

The aftermath of nonviolence
is the creation of the beloved community,
while the aftermath of violence is tragic bitterness....
[A]nother element that must be present in our struggle that
...makes our resistance and nonviolence truly meaningful...
is reconciliation.
Our ultimate end must be the creation of the beloved community.
--Martin L. King Jr.

To move towards the beloved community, people must do things differently. They have to acknowledge that actions do not occur in isolation since what is done in one area affects other areas. To gain solutions to complex challenges today, we have to shift basic assumptions and understandings of relationships, connections, prediction and control, since they are constantly changing qualities. This requires faith since we can't see connections, but we need to know they exist.

...as we look for meaningful and lasting solutions,
there is a lot to learn and unlearn.
These conversations are going to be challenging
- even uncomfortable- but they're important.
Because this time, we get to rebuild America together. Don Lemon

During this pivotal time in history, many more people need to choose to make changes for the collective good. Listen and discuss Don Lemon's podcast with your loved ones. This can benefit our children and families, schools, jobs, communities and our nation – and even globally. We have a deep racial divide in our nation (Don Lemon) that also includes a caste division (I. Wilkerson)

"...Why? Because we're selfish."...
the pandemic ...
has exposed hidden fragilities in American society
[It] ... has also held a mirror
to our national identity, laying bare ...deeply ingrained
individualism has become in our psyche. ...
we must also acknowledge this epidemic of individualism —
an illness that can't be cured with social distancing.—Amin Aalipour

Myths from the past have come with us into the 21st century, like the rugged individual who made it all on his own. That didn't happen then and it doesn't happen now. Sure, centuries have passed in our nation and some individuals continue to be baffled by our actions.

Some things that are bothersome may be unspoken topics that are encountered, like family secrets or policies that seem to say one thing but really do the opposite. Or terms like right to work, when it only benefits the company and not the employee. They're there but polite people don't bring them up. They're secrets even though in-your-face problems sometimes occur as results of past and present actions around them. We have to learn to face them.

We are not held accountable for what happened before we were born, but we need to do better as we know better.

We have a lot on our national, family and school plates. Our nation is losing ground when compared to other advanced industrialized countries. Among them, we have the highest high school drop-out rate in the world; we are number one in children living in poverty and we have higher infant mortality rates. The United States is the first country that ever used the atomic bomb on another country – two times. Now we can add that we have more deaths and covid-19 cases than any other country.

We have more jailed people than any other country in the world. As other things did, policing took different paths in the north and south (Gary Potter). In the north, they started as paid constables to watch over volunteer watchmen, paid by fees for warrants with other non-law enforcement duties. In the south police started as slave patrols using vigilante-style groups to chase and return the enslaved to their owners, to provide organized terror to keep revolts down and to maintain discipline for violating plantation rules.

They later became southern police departments, controlling freed laborers and segregation. As cities grew north and south, police departments grew, but their function was more to keep disorder down as they reacted against disgruntled workers in factories and agriculture using corrupt and brutal forces. Today's policing is a continuation of centuries of brutality.

We also have problems with increasing stress, health concerns and major problems with how we treat and engage with families and others. The present disease pandemic elicits fear in some people to protect their families at all costs. Others may figure that life is bad, so another disease won't make that much of a difference. Sheltering in place has its problems, especially if you have no home and to a lesser degree when family members lived separate lives. Spending unplanned time together in close quarters has caused problems as parents and children try to work on the same digital tools with no scheduled relief. We are definitely not dressed to impress!

Recent presidential campaigns illustrate tendencies that don't bode well for our democracy. They brought to the forefront the extreme polarization of voters, rudeness towards people with opposing views and failures to focus on important issues. Plus, one-sided and factually wrong information seem to be accepted by too many citizens as truth. Civic responsibilities have declined with voter participation that's lower than in most developed countries, participation in local community activities has declined and jury service has declined for various reasons

The U.S. is a representative democracy where citizens elect representatives from among themselves who are supposed to work for the people who elected them. But we have too many life-long politicians and lobbyists of big businesses who make money off the people. Even companies that pay no taxes wind up getting refunds. A party known for keeping government small and prices down while not supporting a former president now has the largest national deficit and many in government who lie outright with fake news.

We move from one crisis to another, not learning lessons from history to resolve problems with sustainable (able to be maintained at a certain rate) solutions. We hope that the last crisis will end, and better economic times will trickle down to our families again with higher standards of living. We feel we have the right to not wear masks and social distance, thinking that "they" will get the virus, but "we" won't. No matter the political party, age or location, covid19 and severe weather due to climate change do not discriminate – but actions around race do discriminate!

Where will we go to make sense of the following connected issues that need solutions? Our children are hurting and these hurt too:

1. Many people search for solace, well-being and wellness in liquor or drugs, sex or extreme behaviors rather than changing how they live. Lifestyle changes will help them develop to feel more hopeful while they work for better selves, families, schools, communities and world relationships.

2. Our foods, bodies, health and planet are compromised by legal chemical innovations. They impact obesity, climate change, unclean air (which may impact the pandemic), toxins exposures and too many food allergens. We emphasize dis-ease and drugs and not enough prevention and wellness while vaping has taken the place of cigarettes, but they also kill. The pandemics add other layers of more stress and illness.

3. Our culture pits the haves and the have-nots against each other, and some families are uncertain which group they belong to or should support since more than income determines the haves. The middle class is shrinking, and part time jobs mean paying for college for a many years.

4. "White" immigrants from Europe who finally lost their accents don't want today's immigrants of color to be in the country. So, should "whites" also go back to their countries of origin as immigrants? Too many immigrant children are forced to work in dangerous industries today, even with child labor laws. Caring for people seems to be decreasing.

5. Some call for "good" Americans, even teachers, to carry weapons for protection and mass killings are too frequent across the nation, even in schools. Guns are not regulated as needed and some are carried in public places by people with mental health problems, quick tempers and/or vigilante behaviors. Police patrol streets with proactive policing to fill prison cells for low-cost labor and sometimes kill with no mercy.

6. Bias is prevalent, and as attempts are made to overhaul police departments, university departments like sociology, education and social work also need to look at their roles in the school to prison pipeline.

7. Injustices and unfair zero tolerance policies are allowed in education: some kindergarteners with temper tantrums are handcuffed; the school to prison pipeline is started with 3rd grade reading difficulties; too many students are unfairly pushed out of school with suspensions and expulsions which lead to future dropouts; and some parents are arrested for seeking better schools for their children.

8. Some of us are shaken in our faith and spirituality with the lack of trust in some unethical and unprincipled ministers and church goers who seem to support popular wrongdoing. Benjamin Franklin and Carter G. Woodson, centuries ago, wrote about this so they are not just current events!

9. Too many of us see, hear, and speak no evil, though support it by being avid viewers, story tellers and participants since some of our favorite actors and politicians do it, too! Is it right or wrong? Do we even care?

10. Some of our children rank extremely low in social emotional well-being and some adults do too. Mental health problems are too prevalent among our children. Poverty, race and social class are said to explain some of this, but it cuts across these areas. Social media impacts our children and adults with addictions to media screens. Largely ignored is the responsibility to change society so it benefits all children and adults, too!

11. Too many farmers, young men and women and some children are committing suicide. Some children are bullied and hated for being

themselves. Too many adults are killing their children and too many children hurt themselves and each other with guns that are more readily available than jobs. Violence needs to be replaced with love, peace and the beloved community.

12. Actions against bullying need to be wider spread to include racism, bias and white supremacy. These actions need to be part of the school curriculum from kindergarten to college for adults and students, too, but lies are being told to distort history, ban books and even libraries.

13. Some of our children and some adults don't like to read though they read screen devices much of the time. Some schools seem confused over how to teach reading which is a need, not an elective, so some people don't read well. Negative attitudes about reading can cause some skills to be lost over time. Some jobs are lost or never gained when employers look at social media postings that show too much skin and poor judgement.

14. Too many people seem unable to cope with life's ordinary demands and routines, possibly with the beginnings of mental illnesses that could start with minor physical, psychological or emotional problems. Get help! Too many children are placed in harm's way and need to be kept safe.

15. We use quick fixes for short time periods when long term commitments by education, government, families, and work are needed to reduce problems that impact well-being, wellness, quality of life and finances.

Many of the above 15 points are issues related to relationships. Today so much is going on in our country. There are many technological innovations and new gadgets that keep some from paying attention to disconnects and breakdowns in families, other relationships, society, schools, and work. At the same time our nation seems to try to go backwards to olden days that limited and excluded people who were different from the majority if they had money and power. With the pandemic we had to depend on technology but need to connect more with nature and other people at a masked safe distance.

The question that needs to be raised: are we learning lessons from the past for a better tomorrow and our collective right to life, liberty and the pursuit of happiness for all the people? We can't leave these issues to politicians from any of the parties since they all seem the same when it comes to people issues in our country. The history and present actions of both major political parties are problematic. Some families' lives are falling apart, and some national choices can make you wonder if our nation is beginning to fall apart also! Think of Rome and Greece that both fell....

Lives fall apart when the foundation
upon which they were built needs to be re-laid.

> *Lives fall apart,*
> *not because God is punishing us*
> *for what we have or have not done.*
> *Lives fall apart because they need to...*
> *they weren't built the right way*
> *in the first place.*
> *--Iyanla Vanzant*

Consumerism. A major misconception and unspoken issue at the heart of what we do in our country is consumerism. Consumerism is the theory that an increasing consumption or use of goods is economically desirable in our capitalist economic system. People have to buy since it helps the economy. No one talks about it- but just buy it! It may be in the back of people's mind that too much of the latest and most expensive are bought when the old is still good, but many figure that everybody else is doing it, so they do, too! Add to that the essential workers who put their lives on the line to keep the country running in agriculture and transportation industry. Families are evicted when they can't pay bills while the cost of housing continues to escalate, forcing more people into the streets.

Too many families have low incomes (even military families are on food stamps) and more with middle incomes are joining them. Our buying mentality leaves many with nowhere to go. We can't continue with our heads in the sand about relationships and efforts to buy happiness. From producers in the past, we have become a nation of consumers who deplete natural resources while generating a lot of waste that harms our Earth's oceans and lands. Are many of us on the train to nowhere with our spending habits?

Some make decisions heavily influenced by the unknown "Joneses" and aggressive business marketing. Many put blinders on as they spend with credit cards, coupons, rewards and discount stores on every corner for spending more while earning less. What is being done now impacts the next generation.

But something different is happening in the second decade of his new century, in addition to the pandemics. Nationally, many children in this generation will not earn more money than their parents' generation for the first time since the founding of our nation. A contradiction with this is that many people are used to a lot of things that cost a lot of money and some jobs are not filled due to lack of skills and drug problems.   Now throughout our nation, laborers are striking and picketing for fair work laws and higher salaries. They saw another way to work during the pandemics and want fair laws for better lives.

The contradiction in consumerism is that human needs must be met since people are more than just consumers. People have physiological or bodily needs for nutritious foods, shelter, clothing and clean air and water, security and protection and they cost money too. People also need relationships for love and a sense of belonging, recognition and status.

When people don't believe in themselves, they are more apt to focus on pleasure and meeting selfish desires, so they feel in control of something. This is done even at the expense of their children's needs and family well-being at times, as seen in recent opiate addictions. Spending money on the latest advertised whatever, over-stimulating senses and emotional eating can become ways of life that help people feel better for a while until their health suffers…or addictions can start.

---

*Use **the 6 W's** for the rest of the book to learn more, then return to the front.*
Who? What? When? Where? Why? and How?
These 6 simple investigative questions are also good when you're speechless in any situation or with any age group. Try it!

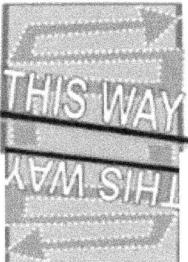

Then they may rob Peter to pay Paul, yet again. Some people feel the pressure and stress in their lives since they may value things more than faith. They may not consciously think about how their choices and decisions impact health, wellness, well-being and their quality of life. It impacts adults but also children's present and future lives. Some people even act as if they don't know what's right or what's wrong because of the decisions they repeatedly make.

It's good that many people are still doing the best that can be done through spiritual practices, improving themselves and reaching out to help others. Many gain satisfaction from working and producing things, and many more people are still interested in working on human possibilities with the ideals of fairness, freedom, participation, social relations and living in harmony with nature and each other that are so needed.

Your parents may have undermined or supported your family's well-being with lifestyle choices, and you may have learned from them. Choices have to be made. Do you want your lifestyle during pandemics to continue as it is, or do you see areas needing change? Hopefully you will take the time to think, feel and know that balance is needed in personal, family and national life.

Again, you're not in this alone. Many people have to deal with themselves so they can move on to better ways of living and learning together with others!

People are ... immobilized because
they cannot imagine an alternative.
We need a vision that recognizes
that we are at one of the great turning points
in human history
when the
survival of our planet
and the restoration of our humanity
require a great sea change in our
ecological, economic, political, and spiritual values.
--Grace Lee Boggs

What are you doing to be more positive? Answer YES or No.

1. Are you trying to stay away from social media at times to relieve stress?

2. Are you going outdoors more to get needed fresh air and sunshine?

3. Are you cooking together with those at home and eating more healthily?

4. Have you planted a flower or a garden to relieve stress?

5. Are you trying to exercise and do yoga for all ages in zoom or in person?

6. Have you started meditating and praying more to relieve stress?

7. Are you reading more? Are you reading humor to laugh more?

8. Are you reaching out to more family and loved ones now?

9. Are you improving and empowering yourself and your children?

10. Are you paying attention to your mental health and the mental health of your your children? Are you reaching out to helping professionals? Are you following influencers with obvious mental health problems?

11. Is your faith growing towards the light and love or darkness?

12. Are you more negative than in the past? Have you tried to figure out why?   Are you lying to yourself and others more?

13. Are you being discerning and fact-checking the news or social media to determine if its fake news, facts or bias, using factcheck.org, Truth or Fiction, PolitiFact or Snopes.com? Or do you stick with what's popular even though it may not make sense or add up?

14. Are you stuck? Go back through some areas of this book to get unstuck.

Work to increase YESes and lessen NOs and you WILL be okay!

Part III: Schooling and Quality of Life

Economic prosperity and quality education
for our children are inexorably linked.
--Jon Huntsman, Jr.

Schooling and quality of life are intertwined. As an adult, you've experienced this fact. Schools and families need to continually change to keep up with the times to improve the quality of living and functioning within society. Schools call their changes reforms, while families sometimes empower themselves to transform, renew or improve. Education gained through schooling is important to the functioning of families and our nation.

Progress on the social ladder is almost always
the result of progress in other areas of your life. –*Oscar Auliq-Ice*

When economic prosperity and quality education come together, personal lives can improve. When people are not adequately educated because of the visible aspects of racial or ethnic discrimination, it's hard to gain better jobs, housing, medical care and even nutritious foods. Some consider these as personal problems, but for centuries our federal government and local policies have controlled housing, jobs, schooling, health and food access. These are political problems since they relate to government and our nation.

This political practice maintains the status quo and makes too many families vulnerable and impoverished. It can also work to keep people negative and set in their ways if they feel dissatisfied or disgruntled about national changes that may superficially help others, especially if fear and anger exist. Life today seems filled with fear and anger as people lash out as we leave behind the major pandemic threats of 'rona and social protests, though work protests are hitting more areas.

When we woke up on the 12th of March 2020, none of us thought that schools and businesses would close with the pandemics the very next day. Stay at home edicts and struggling for necessities caused a lot of stress in addition to the unknown virus. Then we see the ending of Black lives in real time and severe weather on our many screens. Effects of that period are still lingering. Something has to give or take!

In all realms of life it takes courage to stretch your limits,
express your power, and fulfill your potential...
it's no different in the financial realm. –*Suze Orman*

9. Empowerment is the First Step

*It's imperative that ... mindsets stay strong ... clear ... powerful
as one global community, and as individuals.
...[S]elf-care, self-awareness, and personal mastery
are key and critical.
We are at a changing point in society
...what we do ... how we show up
will have a lot to do with the history ... created.*
Lisa Nichols

To get to the point of clear and strong mindsets, many people have to work on themselves while becoming aware of skills they need to improve. This comes through empowerment that takes work. If you like where you are right now and don't want to take efforts to improve, then empowerment is not for you. But think seriously about what you are doing today that could improve for a better tomorrow. None of us are perfect and all of us can improve!

Empowerment is the process of becoming more confident and stronger by taking control of your own life. People need a positive sense of self where they believe in themselves. A positive sense of self includes self-efficacy (being capable), self-confidence (personal worth), self-discipline (will power), self-respect (value self), self-concept (beliefs about self), self-image (mental picture of your body) and self-love (trust that you can love yourself and others can and will love you, too). A sense of self connects the social and emotional sides of being so they can heal inside to relate better with others.

To become empowered, focus on what can be controlled. Be hopeful by trying to display positive attitudes, be willing to learn more and be committed to change in needed areas. When empowered, it's easier to make paradigm shifts to become part of the solution rather than feel victimized and powerless.

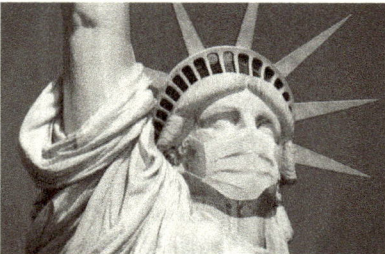

With empowerment should come personal responsibility and commitment that are needed to do something. Journaling started with this book is a part of that commitment, but you have to keep writing in it. Learn more about yourself, learn to connect better with others and believe in yourself!

As attention moves swiftly from fighting for our lives due to the coronavirus, racial unrest and extreme weather, you may want to look at larger systemic changes needed in our nation. You may feel you don't need anything else to change...but...change is happening here and all around the world. Will you be a victim to change? Or will you use information from your story and this book to empower yourself to move from just reading and writing to personal actions, too? It's up to you!

Many steps are needed to change or understand more - whether you want to understand yourself and your family better, how our country got to this point, or want to understand racism and how to move away from it, or how to get out of the poverty mindset or how to change our climate. This is a process to take personal actions that are needed to prove to yourself and others your commitment to change – if you're there.

You've seen people who say they want to save the earth, but never recycle. Or they show up at demonstrations, but you see and feel their discomfort in being around people of other cultures. Or organizations that supposedly help people get out of poverty but never include them in policy discussions and don't show respect for them.

If we want different outcomes to huge problems, people have to change themselves as they change society. Change is a conscious choice to participate in difficult struggles and it needs to and can happen on different levels. The pandemic is changing the way we live, and we need to take this time to develop a common vision for tomorrow. This section will look at some of the skills needed to empower ourselves for change.

We cannot change unless we survive
but we will not survive unless we change.
-- Franklin Greenwald

Commit to humanity for peace.   Humanity is all human beings, all peoples collectively or humankind. It is the state of being human and humane with compassion and civility. When committing to humanity, people acknowledge wanting to work together collectively to address real differences. Peace is tranquility or freedom from disturbance, a period of no war or freedom from worry and anxiety. Humans thrive when peaceful.

When you find peace within yourself,
you become the kind of person who can live at peace with others.
–Peace Pilgrim

It's hoped that people can lay weapons of harsh words, meanness, hate and violence down to discuss differences in families and with others. They need to move from debate (to prove others wrong without focusing on emotions or feelings) to discussions (conversations about topics) to dialogue (listening, then working together towards common understandings). Try to move towards peaceful resolutions to difficult conversations and situations.

This process takes time, but it can be done. Dialogue is needed to seek resolutions, not just debate or discussions. Learning about how people work together in society is a good start to solutioning. Check out Harro's cycle of socialization to understand how oppression and power work together. It illustrates the process that begins with childhood and continues throughout life as people learn to function in society. The cycle explains socialization and how it works.

> *Why is nonviolence such an important philosophy?*
> *Because it respects the capacity of human beings to grow.*
> *It gives them the opportunity to grow their souls.*
> *And we owe that to each other.*
> *And it took me a long time to realize that.*
> *[but she lived until she was 100!] --Grace Lee Boggs*

Human beings can grow and it's easier when they make sense of life. Life always involves relationships. Work is needed to make relationships work toward peace and peace of mind, no matter where or how we interact with others. During these stress-filled times peace is needed in all instances – whether you choose to stay at home alone or among loved ones, demonstrate in the community, or help colleagues learn new skills to work with each other in fairer ways. Peace is needed within ourselves, in our families, community, nationally and globally. When peaceful, empowerment cam grow! Try the following eight areas.

> *Peace is not absence of conflict.*
> *It is the ability to handle conflict by peaceful means.*
> *–Ronald Reagan*

1) Build relationships. Relationships are needed to work on common goals, even if people don't really like each other. To build new relationships or improve them, work peacefully together throughout the process. Be friendly as connections are made; ask questions; tell about yourselves; go places; do things together and accept others as they are. Always pay attention to others, communicate openly and show appreciation. Rather than fear rejection, assume that others want positive relationships with you, be persistent; get involved and enjoy the company of others. It takes time to build and sustain relationships or to keep them going, but it's worth it!

When mistakes are made in building relationships, just try something different. It also helps to get out of personal comfort zones at times, so volunteer to meet and help others, challenge each other to do better and back each other when things get tough. Relationship building is a major area to better engage children with their families, families with school personnel and throughout the community. Technology, programs and policies reinforce relationships, but they can't replace the work needed to build relationships. It can be challenging since social fragmentation seems to be the norm at times, even before the pandemic. Isolation hurts so take this time to reach out to others, however you can!

2) Meditate and pray. In today's hypervigilant internet world, we are center stage to many atrocities and extreme behaviors in real life, on the news and on many screens as entertainment. This causes even more people to be stressed. Physical and mental health problems can increase if we allow too much stress into our lives. We need to be diligent in helping ourselves and others calm down through meditation and prayer. Prayer helps relieve stress while increasing faith. Study the words of your faith and try to spend time intentionally studying it. Grow closer to your Supreme Being by praying consistently at set times of the day in your own way.

Mindfulness meditation is one of many different types of meditation. It started with Buddhism, but anyone can use it. Meditation is good for you and others around you so you may want to try it at home today. Studies have shown it can reduce prison violence, help with work productivity and even improve children's grades and behavior. Meditation can reduce blood pressure, boost recovery after stressful periods, strengthen the immune system, help your brain with aging and lessen anxiety and depression. When coupled with yoga, exercise and movement happen too. Give peace a chance!

3) Begin to heal trauma experienced during this surreal period or from life in general. You know your history. Did your family's past actions or the way you were treated traumatize you? With so much happening with social isolation, you've probably cried more than usual. These tears help people of all ages heal. The emotions that need to be processed with trauma include anger, sadness, shame and fear. These emotions are painful and not socially acceptable, so the process of releasing trauma doesn't happen easily. These emotions can stay with you and eventually affect relationships, jobs, happiness, health and everything else. When you process trauma, you can heal and begin to feel your feelings.

Brandt (2018) recommends dealing with an easy trauma first by doing the following to ground the pain and release it. Then try to heal traumas related to the pandemics. The process will feel strange, but it will work. Try it!

a)   Recall something that provoked a reaction and imagine yourself there.
b)   Sense it by breathing deeply, relax, then observe any physical response.
c)   Give a name to the emotion. Love it and accept the feeling (say I love myself for feeling....”). Feel and experience the emotion.
d)   Receive the message from the past and journal about your feelings.
e)   Share it with someone close or write about reactions and lessons learned.
f)   Write letters to those who hurt you (but don’t send them).
g)   Then let it go by safely burning the letter!

4) Change negative mindsets and be more proactive rather than just reactive. Minds may be set in relation to poverty, relationships or any other mindset that is heavy, hurtful and problematic. Be proactive by working on things before they become problems, if possible. If not, stop right then, schedule a serious meeting, and talk about mindsets.

If getting out of poverty is important as you’re working to empower yourself, consider some different actions that may gain quicker results. The poverty mindset or other mindsets can stay with some people even when their situations change. It can sabotage moves toward better times with thoughts and actions that don’t show positive growth. Sometimes it can show up as a lack of ambition, pessimism and self-pity, with decision-making based on fear and a focus on what you don’t have.

Long-standing cycles need to be broken to make sense of change. Be aware of reactions to situations that cause negativity in words or actions. Consider changing surroundings when negative by going outside to look at nature, pray or meditate, look at the bigger picture, look deeper at where the discomfit really lies, and try to find something humorous in the situation. When poverty is the topic, try to change how money is viewed while being grateful for what you have. Learn to relax as plans are made to work towards new goals and remember to take care of your health and sanity. Most importantly, take responsibility for your actions and don’t give up. This entails another process that has to be worked on!

A note of caution - in this period of scams and frauds in unlikely places, more thought needs to go into choices that are made about things of importance. People need to be more discerning even with formerly trusted companies and community organizations that propose that X will make life better, but then it doesn’t really happen. On-line information is even more problematic as contradictory information has to be researched.

If reaching out to helping professionals or someone contacts you on the internet, check it out. Data is readily available in public reports, so check online or ask organizations for proof that they are doing what they say they will do. Read and discuss the data with others and talk with people who used those services if you haven't used them yet. Don't continue using services just because you did in the past.

Companies should be held **accountable** to do what they say they will do, whether they are stores or social welfare agencies. If they don't, then clients or customers need to get together with other clients to begin to make positive differences. You can go elsewhere if there's a selection of agencies with better track records. Or advocate for better services with the same organizations. This is a long process, but improved services and outcomes might be the result of standing up for change. Try it!

In addition to different types of financial assistance, to get out of poverty people need a good education (so schools need to change and community learning needs to be broadened), changing mindsets toward money (so financial literacy needs to be taught better in schools and in the community); take upgraded skills for 21st century needs); and avoid predatory payday loans (so people need to make a decent living wage so they don't have to use them as alternatives). The same applies to other hurtful relationships.

Your housing situation. You may have had to move in with your parents or friends due to sheltering in place and losing your source of income – with or without children. Space may be tight but be proactive and as positive as possible since tempers can flare with the extra stress. For that arrangement to work intentional plans need to be made so you both can "stay in your lane" in this new arrangement of adults forced to live together. Or you may have been with your parents for a while due to the college bills you are paying, major life changes or whatever.

How has it been for you?

I didn't get there by wishing for it or hoping for it, but by working for it. *--Estee Lauder*

This is written for adult children who have to move back home, but the information may be useful to adults living with adults without children, too. Just ignore childhood information. Both of you need to think about independent lifestyles and how you live now or lived before the pandemic. Make sure that you protect your time, your place and your space, if possible.

You love your adult children or friends but they are now really guests in your home.

If they moved in a while ago, schedule an important meeting to make changes, if needed. They may be friends with problems and you may decide to help each other come out of this period more positive. With covid-19, older parents, grandparents and other loved ones with health problems have to still think about protecting their health. Wearing masks is optional but individuals need to determine what they need to do for themselves. Hold important conversations to keep everyone safe in the household before problems occur if possible.

You want your home to be a peaceful multi-generational one. When young adults are ready for adulting, or behaving as responsible adults, the following rules may also come in handy as they prepare for their futures. Plus they may like a copy of *My Child, Our Future (2ⁿᵈ ed., Vol. 2)* if they have children, or even their personal copy of this book. Try the following that may help:

1. Be upfront with what you expect of adults in your home. They need responsibilities with consequences so you are not raising them again if they're your children. Discuss this before they move in or make tough decisions to not allow them to move in.   Create lists of all household responsibilities. Divide the list with expectations that everyone carries their fair share with rules and penalties for not following the rules.

    Part of that includes pitching in money for household expenses, not just spending money on their own expenses. Money also needs to be saved in a bank or credit union. Learn about financial literacy, if needed.

2. Set rules for adult sleepovers and celibacy while being guests in parent's or friend's homes, and show good judgment. If you live in a small area, this can cause discomfort so go for a walk or outside as the weather changes. Plus, limit your visits with others and limit guests to your home. By now the rules of physical distancing and masks may have changed. If not, continue to protect others and yourself.

3. Make sure adults keep journals and develop action plans for gaining skills and breaking old patterns, if needed, when the time is right to leave home (possibly again). You and your house guests may want to use this time to improve something about yourselves, working together or alone. Review and discuss lessons on critical thinking and decision making from this book. If there's a lack of understanding, dialogue together.

    Hold each other accountable for improving where you are to where you want to go by using critical thinking, financial and wise decision-making skills. This book and the *Occupational Outlook Handbook* are useful for changes in career paths. Use preferred browsers to find articles that relate to them. Public libraries may be open by now, or if not open, books can still be checked out by appointment. Work on other issues so solutions can be sought towards moving on.

4. If returning adult children bring their children (your grandchildren, great-grands etc.) into your home, make sure that they raise their children not you. Suggest that they use *My Child, Our Future* as a guide. Children should also conform to house rules. If older high school children are acting like adults they need these rules too so you can help them to be responsible almost adults as they begin adulting under your roof (if you allow that). Paying part of the adult expenses helps, but make sure they have real jobs and are not doing illegal things to "earn" money.

5. Brainstorm with each other about the skills needed for becoming an entrepreneur if possible. Check out the free and low-cost social media offerings about changing jobs, check YouTube and internet sites with professionals. Consider internet-based jobs so you know what's available. Don't just listen to social media and news – learn more to improve yourself while waiting for life to open again. Be ready!

If your adult move-in does not want to help with expenses, house rules, household chores (or whatever is possible during the pandemic), or skills improvement or protecting others' health, then it may be best that your adult child or friend and you make the decision that they not live in your home. It's your house and your time for peace that you've earned. You don't want to be held hostage by out-of-control adult guests, though I know you may worry about your next generations in their families! If you need another level of defense, read articles about elder abuse, then act.

5) Racial identity and diversity awareness. Your identity is important during this stressful period, no matter your age. Identity is who you are, and it includes the way you think about yourself. You learn your identity from your parents, peers and how the world views you. During this period of racial tensions, you may want to learn more about your racial identity as a starting point for your growth as a human being who is concerned about others.

People need to make a commitment to larger issues by first becoming aware of self. The charts on Diversity Awareness and Racial Identity Development on the next pages can help readers identify where they stand. The awareness survey needs quick answers related to recent experiences. Racial identity informs where you stand as a whole at this particular time. It's a hierarchal chart of stages that people go through as they become who they want to be.

After completing the surveys, examine where you are in life, or where you were at the beginning of the book, and where you are now. Learn more as you delve into survey information as you come across it. Are you more aware? Are you behaving differently the stages of development, or do you have arrested development and have to take a break for awhile?   Share the surveys and discuss results with your friends and family to see where they stand. You'll more readily be able to see some of the collective changes that are necessary as we become the change we seek in the 21st century.

What do you feel and think about what you've read so far?

Is it what you expected?

Is it helping at all in making sense of today? Why and how?

Return to this page after reading and completing the next two surveys. Debrief here!

Diversity Awareness – A Personal Survey *Author Unknown. This scale was first used by Dr. Mapp in the 1980s* *(1) Circle the number closest to your thoughts and feelings* **As an individual, how often do I:**	Seldom/Never	Occasionally	Usually	Mostly/Always
1. Confront or challenge others when they make offensive comments that are racial, sexual, income based or ethnic?	1	2	3	4
2. Confront or challenge others when they make fun of others because of differences in race, gender, religion, appearance?	1	2	3	4
3. Think about the impact of my comments before I speak out or act – and possible consequences due to my comments?	1	2	3	4
4. Refuse to tell derogatory jokes about any group/ individual?	1	2	3	4
5. Refrain from repeating hurtful comments or rumors?	1	2	3	4
6. Avoid generalizing behaviors or attitudes of one individual to the entire group (e.g. "all" men are…)	1	2	3	4
7. Accept that I am biased and understand that my biases can be shown in my actions or words?	1	2	3	4
8. Avoid using language that reinforces negative stereotypes (e.g., You are acting like a …)	1	2	3	4
9. Make an effort to learn about people different from myself (read, attend voluntary seminars, listen to speakers, etc.).	1	2	3	4
10. Support, understand and take responsibility to help my organization and family be inclusive and fair?	1	2	3	4
11. Value people different from me as resources because of their unique skills, abilities, perspectives or approaches?	1	2	3	4
12. Work to make certain that I respect different cultural beliefs and religious holidays?	1	2	3	4
13. Challenge the ideas that individuals need to act or look a certain way to be successful, valuable and feel included?	1	2	3	4
14. Forgive people who make offensive statements about others or me and allow them to regain my trust and respect?	1	2	3	4
15. Invite and include diverse people into decision- making?	1	2	3	4
16. Provide timely and honest feedback to others, including those different from me, even if it feels uncomfortable?	1	2	3	4
17. Willingly share written and unwritten rules of my workgroup with colleagues different from me for a level playing field?	1	2	3	4
18. Support workplace policies regarding equal/fair treatment by confronting people who violate policies and report them?	1	2	3	4
19. Get to know people of different races as individuals (make first efforts to talk to them, invite them to socialize, etc.)?	1	2	3	4
20. Listen, try to understand, be aware of our history, display cultural humility and be more culturally humble?	1	2	3	4

(2).Now add the scores for 1-20 above for your **Total Score** *here>.*

If everyone's thinking alike, then someone isn't thinking--G.S. Patton

Diversity Awareness Survey Results	*Your Total Score:*

1 - - 20 points	You need work since you are out of touch with others. You really need to get out of your comfort zone.
21 – 40 points	You are a perpetuator of the status quo and prefer no change.
41 – 59 points	You are an avoider
60 – 78 points	You can be a diversity change agent.
79 – 84 points	You are a fighter for diversity with in-your-face points and you have what it takes to be an advocate!

(3) Where are you on Diversity Awareness? Circle it in the above Result.
(4) Did you think your scores would be different? _____
(5) Do you have work to do or are you where you'd like to be? _____ *Why?*
Use another sheet of paper to record this most important information!

Racial Identity Development

(1).Select Your Race or Ethnicity (A or B). For longer explanations, see
https://www.racialequitytools.org/resourcefiles/CompilationofRacialIdentityModel

A) *African Americans and Other People of Color (*Cross, '87; Gay, 00)

Your Stage of Development	*Short Description*
Pre-encounter	Pro-White, anti-Black or another ethnicity
Encounter	Pro-Black/Black/another ethnicity, anti-White
Immersion/Emersion	Intensely focused; pro-Black/other ethnicity
Internalization	Resolves conflicts with worldviews
Internalization-commitment	Commitment to sharing with other races

B) *European Americans* (Helms, 1990; Tatum, 1997)

Your Stage of Development	*Short Description*
Contact	Little attention to race-identity + importance
Disintegration	Growing awareness of racism/privilege
Reintegration	Conflict now; fear and anger re color
Pseudo-independent	Race aware and self-conscious
Immersion/emersion	Less guilt but need antiracist Whites
Autonomy	Racial self-actualization/confront racism

(2) Circle your stage of development. Were there any surprises?
(3) As you go through this book, your stage of development may change
(4) *Check out Singh, A. A. (2019).* Racial Healing Handbook: Practical Activities to Help You Challenge Privilege, Confront Systemic Racism and Engage in Collective Healing

This information is useful whether you're working to end racist practices or you've been hurt by racism. How do you feel?

6) Choose to let "it" go. Empowerment demands that people let go of some things so their empowered selves can emerge. Whatever the "it" is, it can possibly keep people from expressing pain and/or admitting responsibility. Or "it" may mean letting go of friends who try to keep you down or don't want you to improve. Or let go of the "it" so you can forgive yourself or others.

When a person lets go, it's easier to stop blaming others and stop being a victim. It's then easier to focus on the present. By doing this, you're free to create new goals with positive attitudes, effort and planning or to make sense of your childhood. When people believe they can make a positive difference, it will happen!

7) Choose hope: Another influencer is how people feel about the future. When people can't let go of recent or multigenerational pain or trauma, it hurts them. It also shapes their children's development, academic achievement and how they view the world, so your feelings may come from previous generations. The past cannot be changed. When people cling to it, they can get stuck in it and feel powerless, angry, hurt and victimized.

Check out *There's No Victim Mentality While Fighting White Racism* by Sam McKenzie Jr., or websites: *How to Deal with Racist People*, *How to Be An Anti-Racist*, and Don Lemon's podcasts, *Silence is Not an Option*. Let faith support you as you put gratitude and joy into life while moving beyond barriers that may have started in childhood. Record changes in your journal and continue to grow.

You have to look deeper,
way below the anger, the hurt, the hate, the jealousy, the self-pity,
way down deeper where the dreams lie...
Find your dream.
It's the pursuit of the dream that heals you.
--Billy Mills, Oglala Lakota

Living in the early decades of the 21st century demands: continuous learning, feeling positive, building relationships, thinking critically and planning for the unexpected. It's past time to be serious during this period of rapid changes and instant information. We have to stop and think about the effects of half-truths and partial stories told about our country without the links to the real lives of our families, communities, nation and even the world.

8). Reinvent yourself. Empower yourself to become more confident and stronger while thinking skills and mindsets improve. Look at your friends to determine if they are on the same path as you – then help them join you or let them go. You want to grow into your future in more positive and accepting ways with positive others. Plus remember to keep saving to fuel your dream. Look at where YOU are now... Did you fulfill YOUR dreams from the past, or did "life" change your plans? Use your story and gain the skills you need to move beyond where you are right now as you become the change you desire. Hopefully you've viewed the 15 minute video, *A Future for Us All* by Sir Ken Robinson by now.

Are your skills marketable? Do you have skills, but you are unsure of what they really are?   Take some career quizzes online, check your local adult education or continuing education division or community organization initiatives. Find out your interests or work passions. When you do things in order, you'll find that after graduation or that GED, more opportunities open. Email DrMapp818@gmail.com with "Future" in the subject for a brochure with up to date information.

Survival skills are necessary. Discuss them with other people in your household. Understand, learn about, and use the survival skills that are needed today. They include:
1. critical thinking and problem solving;
2. collaboration across networks and leading by influence;
3. agility and adaptability;
4. initiative and entrepreneurialism;
5. effective and clear oral and written communication;
6. how to access and analyze information; and
7. curiosity and imagination.

Another layer of survival skills are those that are needed to survive in nature. Adults have to participate with children in this activity that will get them outdoors to get some needed fresh air away from screens. Learning new skills together helps children be more satisfied with their home life. Hopefully you did activities outside on multiple occasions during the pandemic. When these skills are used, people can thrive rather than just survive as they make sense of this turbulent period.

Need help in going back to finish that GED or college degree? If your reading and writing skills are a little rusty, call or contact adult education or other initiatives in your county or state on the internet. Read everything to find openings in new jobs that you never trained for. Contact the businesses and find out if they do the training you need to be successful. Find out class locations and write them down in your journal and put on your refrigerator as a reminder. Be creative and keep your eyes and ears alert to view commercials and hear about new jobs that are being created.

Will your job pay for going back to school, especially in an area of need? Ask your human resources director or unemployment counselor who may surprise you if you have a good work ethic! If over 65, you may be able to attend some college courses for free. Libraries may not be full-service, but use them as much as possible and be aware of their schedules. If you have a cell phone, use an old computer screen or television with an adapter to display your cell phone monitor onto the larger viewing screen. Be creative and do something uncommon to help you move to tomorrow.

There are only a few excuses for not taking care of business today!

If you are a veteran, contact the Veterans Administration (VA) or your state higher education agency to find money to pay for college, retraining or to help with other issues like mental or physical health or homelessness. During this pandemic period some businesses may not be open, but don't assume or rely on he/she said. Do the work and check your attitude - get over negatives about wearing uniforms, getting dirty or your friends don't, if that's your work problem! Work is that, then clean yourself up and get paid!

Check this list for other opportunities to help you move to more financial security: (email Support@DrMappSpeaks.com for active links).

1. **On-the-Job Training** – apply to work for a business offering training.

2. **Co-Op Education** –a type of internship program for college students with paid career training as you work and take college courses.

3. **Apprenticeships** – complete a 3-4-year training program that combines on-the-job training with technical and educational instruction.

4. **Private Business or Trade School** – short term training (1 month – 1 year) for jobs like cosmetology or truck driving. Costs vary.

5. **Check trends** (recent changes) and locations in industries that are hiring in areas like mechanical engineering and technology. Use the *Occupational Outlook Handbook* to find trends, then get the training.

6. **Community College** – one semester to two-year school offering vocational and technical programs leading to certificates, diplomas or associate degrees. Save money for two years and get an associate degree, then transfer to a four-year college to complete the bachelor's degree. They offer developmental or high school courses you pay for.

7. **College or University** –a four-year minimum program with entrance requirements based on high school grades (offer developmental courses, too if not fully prepared) and college entrance test scores. Students may apply for application waivers; 4 colleges don't charge traditional tuition.

8. **Some jobs** pay for its workers to go to college. Read and ask HR.

9. **Military** – work for the USA; get training (consider school ROTC), pay, room and board and benefits. Be aware that pay is sometimes for single people, not to support families. For high school or GED graduates only.

10. Programs like the **Job Corps -** a free education and training program that helps low-income teens (at least age 16) learn a career, earn a high school diploma or GED, then find and keep a good job as alternative ed.

11. **Volunteer** with low pay for college students, but many are satisfied with the work experiences that occur in these three settings:

    Peace Corps for college grads or exchange program to give to the world.

    AmeriCorps Volunteers in Service to America/VISTA – an antipoverty program for 17-24-year-old students who are placed in community settings with low budget, but training and work possibilities.

    Student Conservation Associates with jobs and internships (age 18 up).

    Teach for America-a network of leaders who confront educational injustices as corps members teaching in low income schools for 2 years.

12. Check out **infrastructure jobs**: for building and maintaining water pipes, power grids, transit lines, etc. with on-the-job training, possibly higher pay.

13. Try sustainable **agriculture** or agricultural business, including urban farming. Today's majors may include what you need to disrupt patterns.

14. Look at your interests and abilities to become an **entrepreneur or small business owner -** if you have know-how and passion about a hobby or skills and have financing. See Small Business Administration at libraries.

15. **Internships** are programs that provide practical experience for beginners in an occupation or profession to get a foot in door. Some offer stipends.

16. **Cross-industry talent exchanges** – ask your organization if they are doing this exchange which temporarily moves employees without work due to the crisis to organizations needing more workers.

17. **Home based remote jobs** – six needed skills include: ability to work independently, self-motivation, strong written communication skills, comfort in learning and using digital tools, be a team player and have cross-cultural literacy and have reliable and secure equipment. (Flex Job) See https://www.entrepreneur.com/article/306578 for more information.

18. **Miscellaneous info:** Check out findsomethingnew.org and edsource.org; some certificate and diploma programs have placement exams; 8 colleges accept low GPA.

Shoot for the moon.
Even if you miss it, you will land among the stars!
--Les Brown

Reminders: A career is a series of connected jobs in the same area where experiences and networking can lead to additional opportunities. A job is something you do to earn money with possibly little impact on your future work life. Clues or reminders for when you get a job or begin your career: report to work on time; follow work rules; practice good listening; ask questions; dress appropriately; have a positive attitude; be respectful and be flexible. Learn practical tips for finding your passion in life, if needed, and more about What's the Difference Between a Job and Career at indeed.com/career (July 31, 2023).

Clues to *keep* a job or career include: get to work on time; understand your boss' expectations and your role; be professional and keep personal emotions away from work; don't gossip. Show initiative; practice active listening and take notes if you forget easily; be respectful and positive; accept change; learn your weak areas and improve your skills; develop positive relationships; keep work info separate from social media; continuously learn and be flexible.

The way we work is undergoing a fundamental shift. ...
tens of millions of people
are entering the gig economy as
solopreneurs, freelancers, independent consultants, gig workers,
etc. – Entrepreneur Studio Staff Article/ 331635

Get a free white paper at that site on growing and protecting your business. Different skills are needed if you want to become an entrepreneur which is a different mindset from being a worker. Read the *Forbes* article to learn more. The skills include: curiosity, time management, strategic thinking, efficiency, resilience, communication, networking, branding and sales and commitment.

When we strive to become better than we are,
everything around us becomes better too.
—Paulo Coelho

Remember that this is a tight job market in some areas but open in some since undocumented workers remain out of sight. Though it was reported on the news before the pandemic that the U.S. has more people working that at any other time, actual facts and numbers of homeless and certain demographic groups don't support that point.

Some people can't get jobs for many different reasons, and long-term unemployment can be financially, emotionally and psychologically stressful. Lack of work can lead to illness, family problems, depression and desperation. On top of that, unscrupulous people prey on unsuspecting people who need to always beware of scams. It's stressful but choices made can improve your financial security and quality of life. Remember that humans need to work, whether its paid or unpaid. Work is good for health, well-being, confidence, happiness, purpose and financial security.

You read through a lot of information in this chapter.
Hopefully you circled areas you need to work on.
Take time now to either look or relook at the video A **Future for Us All**
for *clues concerning possible interests that relate to your future career/jobs. And or develop a list of things to do under each of these 8 chapter sections.*

You're now on your way to a better future!

10. Overcoming Schooling Gaps

If ...in a hospital, we give you more resources to catch you up,
to make sure you walk out that door...
strong and healthy....
In school it should be the same way.
If you're falling behind,
we should devote more attention to you...
[That's equity!]
-- Ben Jealous

How you were schooled impacts your future earnings and your life. If done right, schooling can make it easier to understand interacting with other cultures and races and how to get out of poverty. Both areas impact individuals, families and society, the satisfaction of work and the importance of taking care of the earth. Many Americans have faith in the power of schooling through education to transform society. Many want it to ultimately help them transform their quality of living and family lives. Thus, schooling gaps impact work and being able to earn a living that families can thrive on.

The U.S. has never had quality education for all. Social and economic inequities have always been intentionally reproduced in our school systems to mirror society since they prepare children to understand society's place for them. When we understand the history of our nation, we can make more sense of the many gaps in schooling and societal success among individuals.

The past is over, but it passed down to 21st century (2000s) generations some problems from the 17th century (1600s) around relationships and how we treat people and Earth. This impacts all humans, our society and the world.

There is a paradox in... PreK–12 schools and ... teacher education.
Parents and teachers want schooling to support children's
ability to become lifelong learners...able to love, work, and act as
responsible members of the community.
Yet, we have not ... integrated these values
into... schools or ... training we give teachers.
-- Jonathan Cohen, National School Climate Center

These differences produce **gaps** as circumstances or obstacles that keep people apart and prevent progress. Many have learned how to make-do with substitutions at times, but the lack of a good education has few substitutes. The gap of not learning enough can have far reaching consequences.

Schooling history. An important fact to mention about inequities in our nation. Few rural (not in cities) southerners of either race went beyond the 8th grade until after **1945**. Just nine years later (**1954**), racially segregated schools were declared inferior to other schools by the Supreme Court in *Brown v. Board of Education* of Topeka. We sometimes wonder why people in certain areas of the country don't seem as smart or advanced as others with more schooling when high schools weren't available locally. Or some may wonder why people nationwide were so angry when their facilities had to be shared with people who were considered as property just a century before.

Education reform continued with a few strategies to keep peace in schools that reluctantly accepted students of color and later consolidated rural schools. Few schools and educators were prepared for the new changes since structural (the organization of schools) and relationship problems in our country were/are still being reproduced in our educational systems.

> *If the vision of educational fairness*
> *expressed in the Brown decision is to be achieved, the*
> *nation must deal with the underlying driver of racial segregation*
> *...the inclination of white citizens to hoard educational resources.*
> *....The historical record shows that the desire ...undermined*
> *desegregation orders ...from 1954 [-] present.*
> *-- Jerry Rosiek*

Desegregation is the process of ending the separation of two races. The battle for desegregation was long and hard across our nation and was fought by many civil rights activists in many cities. We know about Dr. King and other leaders the media sought, but others like James R. Mapp of Chattanooga, Tennessee did their part. He had the nation's longest running school desegregation case before the Supreme Court because of the re-segregation of schools that took place while schools were desegregating. He wrote his memoir before passing and his last words on his 2015 death bed were: "the battle is not over!" Mr. Mapp was my father and in 2023, his words resonate even louder!

> *When it comes to issues of race...*
> *much ignorance and racism persist to this day. ...*
> *We know we must keep the faith and vigilantly work ...*
> *to erase the veil of ignorance....*
> *It is my hope and prayer that ...*
> *young people realize that the battles won*
> *do not signal that the war on racism and injustice has ended.*
> —*James R. Mapp,* Chance or Circumstance? *(jamesrmapp.org)*

Some desegregation changes were positive: there were some reductions in racial prejudice; comfort levels around diverse students increased; and cooperative learning and multicultural education were used for a while. Desegregation has helped to improve some negative academic effects across races. It also raised some income levels and wealth accumulation across generations, as well as health outcomes.

But desegregation also yielded and continues to yield complicated psychological effects that impact some African American children and their learning. When coupled with stressors from home, school and community, learning can be doubly impacted with racism impacting all those areas. Though desegregation balanced some access to resources, some educators still hold implicit and explicit racist attitudes that impact their students. Plus, some children were and are still seen by some as intellectually, and sometimes other ways, inferior.

Even in cities that say they support school integration; many still have barriers that limit access to improved education. This includes school zoning, school policies, segregated classes, housing patterns and neighborhood secessionist policies where small "cities" become entities governing their own schools. Another barrier is the placement of magnet programs in troubled schools that are sometimes run like private schools within public schools. If the magnets were for all students, positive changes can happen.

Schooling progress had been reported for years in national reports, but disparities or differences between student groups were overlooked. They were overlooked until 1986 when the National Alliance of Black School Educators developed a way to look at data. They were able to disaggregate (separate into parts) data to determine gaps in academic achievement among different student demographic groups. This data reported on students from diverse demographic groups located in the census, like race, family income, gender, etc. No longer could differences be overlooked since data now told who was achieving or who was not achieving!

The *education achievement gap* is the difference in achievement between students from diverse groups (BIPOC – Black Indigenous People of Color) compared with European American students. All students were and are not presently achieving academically. Even those who excel in school may not be getting the skills and knowledge needed to improve our 21st century nation and the world.

Around **2000**, the federal government finally held public schools accountable for the academic achievement of all students. Some school districts have been working for more than forty years to close gaps in achievement and they are still working at it. Population shifts have occurred repeatedly in our nation, many times due to economic situations and how people were treated.

During the **2010**s, another major population shift occurred in the growth of the Latinx (the gender neutral term for Hispanic and Latino/a) population and a decline in European Americans. With that and a steady rise in the number of Asian American and multi-racial students with the flat growth of African American students, a former minority has outgrown the majority in some schools and in some parts of the country.

Test scores of some Latinx students have recently risen above some African American students in many schools, even though language barriers are prevalent with some Latinx students. We have a lot of work to do to prepare all students for more successful futures in their personal, public or political lives as they prepare for the future world they will inherit. Also needed is the important work of teaching Americans and other cultures across the world how to live peacefully together in our families, communities, nations and world.

Education gaps also appear in grades, test scores, course selections, dropout rates, college completion rates, suspension rates, course offerings, grade retention rates, attendance in dropout factory schools, lower math and reading achievement, behavioral problems and risk of interpersonal and self-directed violence. These gaps appear in a mix of factors across race, income and family structures, English language proficiency (how well students speak English) and learning disabilities. These gaps persist even when children are in the same class, supposedly receiving the same instruction from the same curriculum.

So, something else is happening in our classrooms!

Differences in achievement levels occur because of complex reasons. Could relationship issues be part of the problem? Most school systems do little to acknowledge bias and prejudged opinions that influence how people act with others, especially in stressful school conditions. Equity and fairness can't be disregarded since they influence how people are sometimes treated, especially in education, a supposed leveling field. Equity and fairness are also needed in work situations since discrimination occurs there also.

In the past, equality or giving all children the same skills not matched to individual needs, was supposedly used. Teachers taught to the "middle" of children's skills, hoping to reach most in the classroom. But later research proved that they were not reaching and teaching most students.

With *equity*, teaching is not delivered to the middle. Students who need the most are given the best teachers, resources and in–and-out-of-school experiences that help accelerate their learning. This cuts across race into poverty that impacts all races of students. If it occurred, children with the least skills, achievement and home preparations would get a jumpstart to catch up to others who start school with more supports, so they do better in school. In many schools, children who need equity are usually remediated or taught low level skills repeatedly. Its better to accelerate their learning and experiences with new information and different ways of learning, not just repeating a grade level the same way again.

> *Empowering Black [and poor] children*
> *is more than teaching them math and reading skills.*
> *They must know how to compete for wealth and power*
> *rather than poverty and acceptance,*
> *to produce rather than consume,*
> *and to be job producers rather than job seekers.*
> *--Claud Anderson*

Some students of all races and incomes have always achieved excellence, attained good jobs, were self-employed and became leaders. This was due to their home lives and perseverance, in spite of formal schooling and the community at times that tried to keep them down. Those who were privileged usually had the best teachers, schools and resources. Many students not in the privileged group were not achieving as well, but that was expected and considered normal. It helped support the US economy by providing a steady stream of industrial and service labor for centuries.

When schools were desegregated, access to housing and jobs away from segregated areas increased. A casualty not considered due to desegregation was the loss of vibrant segregated communities, small businesses and education jobs (including principals who became custodians) over decades. As some people lost jobs in many fields, some eventually stopped looking for work and homelessness and lack of hope grew.

As usual, contradictions still existed. Housing laws still function today in some areas to keep certain people out of or in some neighborhoods, schools and many jobs. It's still prevalent to see just one or two Black workers in many businesses (including some schools) in all levels of income. Frustrated segregated communities with limited job opportunities, schools that don't teach skills that are needed to move ahead nor how to live more peacefully in communities and the world, and inadequate services may influence some recent uprisings in our cities.

Gaps during the last 20 years also grew in skills and behaviors related to *civic engagement* and a lack of social trust among students and adults overall. These behaviors include less participation by some lower-income and middle-income students in volunteering, academic clubs, community participation, extracurricular activities and sports. Self-imposed screen time isolation may keep some students away from positive participation in these areas but something else is happening since many adults don't participate either. Though adults are also addicted to screen time.

> *Yet, some communities have*
> *a strong culture of engagement*
> *where residents, organizations, government and others*
> *recognize and value engagement and*
> *community-decision making....*
> *[They have] fewer intractable problems*
> *and a higher quality of life. ...*
> *[They] experience greater equity,*
> *display greater civic pride   and*
> *exhibit stronger civic responsibility.*
> *--National Civic League*

In many places, it may seem that our nation has been very intent on keeping some people in their "places." That focus should have been on civic participation by everybody since participation is needed in a democracy. This is supposedly one of the missions that schools nationwide are supposed to fulfill. But if taught well with links to consequences today, more students may learn what historical documents really say and they may question the status quo or the way things are now.

We are putting our students' futures at risk since we do not teach them how to interact and live in a democracy. This has unfortunately been happening for generations. Some people are intent on moving us towards authoritarianism, though many of them probably don't even know its definition. They are following negative influencers who attempt to control our nation to protect an individual for choices that were made for decades. They also want to prove that the actions of some of their forefathers and mothers were right even though they were against founding documents and the lives of many people.

You've seen people like that in other countries but this is the first time that such negative actions have been accepted and acted on publicly by so many people in politics, other institutions and by just plain citizens. Authoritarianism is a way of governing that values order and control over personal freedom (except for those in control) through repression and the exclusion of challengers. The leader is a dictator. Political parties and large organizations are used to maintain regime goals which impacts the nation and institutions. Schools are being bombarded now.

School stakeholders are people with an interest in schooling and education. They range from students to their parents and families, to citizens and others with or without children in schools. Stakeholders don't have to accept things as they are – they can connect with others to make sense of schools, critique them and advocate for better schools – and workplaces!

Public schools belong to the public, not just to parents of students.

Schools are a public responsibility. Whether schools need to improve, or not, advocates are needed to make sure that student needs are being met and students are being prepared for their personal futures and the future of our nation. No matter the "quality" of schools their children attend, families can never assume that they are being taught what's needed or treated right, so they have to stay engaged with children's schools until graduation.

Public schooling has gone through many changes as schools were "reformed" over the centuries. Educators are still reforming and learning, which can bring to the forefront more contradictions and misunderstandings with research and reality that may be faulty or unproven. When discomfort around difference is present, as in white privilege, actions need to be taken to get over the discomfort. Sometimes people's hesitancy keeps real change from occurring, possibly evidence of another gap.

Most families give children many chances to improve their skills since they know that children's minds and actions change with practice and age. At school, students usually are tested once to prove their skills. This schooling contradiction was to change with the use of the ***growth mindset*** in the 2015 ESSA (Every Student Succeeds Act) guidelines. But some counties voted against having to show improved student growth.

ESSA took the place of 2002 NCLB (No Child Left Behind). These are law reauthorizations that govern U.S. public education policy under the Elementary and Secondary Education Act of 1965, which had a goal to give federal funds to districts with low-income children to improve educational equity.

Was there success in your district?
Was it for all students or only the same groups that were already achieving?

A growth mindset is a belief that with effort and commitment, people's brains can produce learning and improvements in achievement, like practicing a sport. With the use of the ESSA growth mindset, teachers were to teach differently, and students were to learn to believe they could be successful, but many states decided not to use it. If beliefs and attitudes are open to growth and change, more goals in schools and our democracy can seem attainable. Jobs and higher education are recent goals of ESSA since too many students are homeless and hungry in our nation or can't get good jobs due to a lack of education. But students need more than just college as higher education. They need to be trained beyond high school graduation for certificates and other forms of education connected to well-paying jobs.

We are dedicated to renewing America
by continuing the quest to realize our nation's highest ideals,
honestly confronting the challenges
caused by rapid technological and social change
and seizing the opportunities those changes create.
—New America.org

Soft skills. It is now the 21st century and schools and institutions should be doing things differently for the needs of these times rather than just fulfilling the tried, but not true schooling promises from the past. Education is full of "shoulda, woulda, couldas." Schools should be educating adults (including faculty and staff) and students on how to get along with each other. That includes how to respect others, reduce bias, get beyond racism, dialogue, use citizenship skills and social and emotional skills, how to talk so others will listen, discipline with dignity and other skills needed in a democracy and even in our homes, schools and workplaces. Then teaching all students so they learn and non-discriminatory workplaces will more easily be the norm without bullying.

Families, school personnel and communities should model these positives which are the "soft skills" needed to help children develop in areas of self-discipline, more respect and greater learning. Soft skills are character traits that positively affect how people work and interact with others. They include traits like teamwork, communication, adaptability, problem-solving, leadership, time management and creativity. They were called people skills in the past.

Though not taught as a subject in schools, soft skills encompass *social emotional learning* (SEL, CASEL dot org) which is more than just a program or lesson in school. Some of you were taught to use soft skills or social and emotional strategies by parents and your families. Or some people learned them on their own as they became empowered and more humane.

People need to be self-aware with self-management of emotions while being socially aware with relationship skills and responsible decision making, too. These and other soft skills assist individuals in interacting effectively and harmoniously with others, setting and achieving goals and show empathy. Needed hard skills are technical and work specific, and with soft skills workers and management are   better prepared in business. With soft skills and emotional and social skills, citizens who want to improve democracy for all within the nation are also easier to obtain.

During local, national and international demands for racial justice, ending poverty and environmental change, opportunities to do some things differently are happening. Each person interested in our nation has a responsibility to learn more about what they don't know, personally and in their areas of expertise, along with the behaviors and actions that can help repair and heal our nation.

Equal rights are being demanded as our national story endures questions about our democracy's checkered history. Equal rights is a concept that all peoples should be treated the same under the law. **Civil rights** are nonpolitical rights of citizens to personal liberties outlined in the U.S. Constitution. Schooling in a democracy is a civil right – or should it be an equal right by now? Making sense of the standards undergirding education helps people understand changes that are needed for today. Think about your formal education as you went through school or if you're returning to school or trying to improve your workplace.

Laws influence how schools are run, but the individual states, school systems and schools that impact their day-to-day operations have to pass through another level of policies, school funding and rules.   Events in schools are influenced locally by the direct actions of people – from elected boards to administrators to teachers who teach to parents who send their children to school as students.

Each state has worked on reforming education for centuries. The federal government had to finally lead the way in **1965** because of unfairness, inequities and other problems within the states. As the 20th century was left behind, our nation stumbled into the 21st century as national groups and the government finally worked together to set national standards for education. They are known as ***Common Core State Standards*** (CCSS). More is written about them in ***My Child, Our Future (2nd ed., Vol 2).***

Studying the Social in Learning

Schools should be teaching and modeling social and emotional learning. If not, the school subject that is natural for teaching SEL is Social Studies, which is basically the study of human society. It includes social relationships and the functioning of society which are discussed in this book. It integrates the study of social sciences and humanities (the fact or condition of being human) to promote civic competence, which is the goal of social studies. It should teach the knowledge, thinking processes and democratic attitudes that are required to become active and engaged participants in public life and in relationships at work and home.

If teachers don't understand inquiry and have few soft or people skills, they'll have a deficit before they even start teaching. When children are taught how to live and be in the 21st century world, learning can be easier for them. Unfortunately, many citizens know little about social studies due to how it was taught or who taught it.

During the last 20 years testing in reading and math predominated schools. During the years after 9/11/2001 the social studies profession warred over what should be taught about that event.   Before then, many of our nation's biases restricted learning unless teachers were courageous and knowledgeable about the whole American story.   This problem continues today in some schools.

The Social Studies are important to make sense of the personal and political aspects of living and learning, and the five branches include:

1...History for understanding the past in relation to the present;

2...Citizenship and Government for civic competence;

3...Geography for knowing where people and places are located and their effects on the environment;

4.   *Economics* for understanding how economic systems work (such as capitalism), savings and financial literacy, financial security and

5. *Psychology* and sometimes *Sociology* are added because they both are the scientific study of people, study emotions, relationships and behaviors, from the individual mind to societal behaviors.

Social and emotional strategies help individuals with the soft skills needed to live and participate peacefully in relationships in families, community and society in general. Hard skills are learned through training, based on technical knowledge and industry specific.

Soft skills and social studies skills directly relate to contradictions and misconceptions in our society that impact civility, relationships and even our health and democracy. Connections exist among these areas since they all relate to being human and living peacefully in society with diverse others. Nothing is simple and clear cut. In this fast paced global world, we need to develop into stronger people ready to grapple with issues from the past while building future hope.

We may have
different religions,
different languages,
different colored skin,
but
we all belong to
1 human race.
–Kofi Annan

When you see something that is not right,
you have a
moral obligation
to do something!
... Make Good Trouble!
– John Lewis

The use of soft skills makes work in any profession run more smoothly. You've probably seen colleagues and co-workers who have few soft skills. Hopefully you are not one of them – or if you are, hopefully you're ready to change or adjust.

Which social emotional strategies do you need to learn more about? Why?

.

Check out the Wallace Foundation's free downloads on Social and Emotional learning. .See wallacefoundation.org/promos2/pages/navigating-social-and-emotional-learning.

For adults in workplaces, ties to social intelligence are seen in this area: .inspirus.com/best-practices-for-employee-engagement-and-retention

11. Advocate for Change

I read those reports. . . the 1919 riot in Chicago,
… the Harlem riot of '35, the report of the …Harlem riot of '43,
the report …on the Watts riot [1965]. ..
… the same analysis, the same recommendations
and the same inaction. --Dr. Kenneth B. Clark, 1968

In responding to why the rebellions occurred,
the Kerner Report pointed to black American's
frustration and feelings of powerlessness
regarding extremely high rates of unemployment
and underemployment, poverty, police brutality,
and inadequate public services....
the racism of white Americans was "essentially responsible
for the explosive mixture," leading to the uprisings.
—Kerner Commission, 1968

I was 37 when I served on the (Kerner) Commission, …
Whoever thought that 50 years later,
we'd still be talking about the same things? That's kinda sad.
—Fred Harris, the last survivor of the Kerner Commission Report, 50ᵗʰ anniversary.

From the above quotes, it can be seen that urban rebellions, or protests for racial justice, are not new to our nation. This chapter will help readers build advocacy skills to join together with others to resolve the many contradictions within our country around inequities.

Many injustices need to be worked on towards the ending of behaviors and practices that work against our humanity and the earth that sustains us. Many groups are working to do that. They include Black Lives Matter, People of Color, Eradication of Poverty, Criminal Justice, Social Justice, our Earth, Our Small Farms, Climate Change, Teaching for Change, Small Entrepreneurs, Environmental Justice, and many more.

You and your group may be at the point where you are ready to do something so America lives up to its lofty ideals and needed changes. Or you may be in offices that need to change to conform to lofty mission statements or to injustices brought to light. America needs to change, and you and your family or workplace are part of that needed change. Join together with other groups to advocate for change.

During your life, you possibly used individual advocacy skills when talking to others on behalf of someone or a project. You probably even had to advocate with family members and friends about making changes in your lifestyle as you began to work for more well-being and wellness. So advocacy is not totally new to you in an informal way!

Advocacy is action that speaks in favor or support of various causes, or argues for them, while defending or pleading on behalf of others. It is done to make something else happen to bring about desired changes or outcomes.

Different kinds of advocacy exist: self-advocacy, group advocacy, peer advocacy, citizen advocacy, professional advocacy, non-instructed advocacy and systems advocacy. Systems advocacy hopes to influence the way things are done from a systems point of view for everyone in an entity, school, county, district, state or even country.

Advocates are needed to help improve our families, communities and nation. Schools need constant advocacy since they reproduce national inequalities and contradictions. As a result of reading this guide, you know a little more about history's effects on today's institutions like schooling. Life has changed and schooling tries to benefit our nation but it still doesn't benefit all students.

Advocacy skills include joint voices that form relationships for working together effectively. People gain confidence in skills when they make decisions that may differ from friends, family members or others. Keeping this personal, you may have stood up for what was needed during times of uncertainty. You learned where and how to find information so more informed decisions were made to rectify situations. You may have had to move out of your comfort zone.

You probably used effective communication skills when you talked to children and adults about issues of substance while building trust. Problems were solved and actions were taken while analyzing conditions needing solutions, plus you possibly delegated responsibilities to others. Community resources and agencies were possibly used while networking with others. You may have organized other people and planned actions for success. You applied your skills and experiences and advocated in other areas when necessary.

So, you already have what it takes to be a first-class advocate!

Community Advocacy

As an advocate, experiences, resources and support are shared with other individuals and groups to learn how systems work. You learn public speaking and how to effectively communicate with government officials at times and how to preside over meetings as events are planned. Time and scheduling will create new advocacy pursuits if you wish, or you may just want to learn more about working more effectively with your own community. As seen above, you have advocacy skills that can be used to improve your family, the community, schools and democracy.

Working with others. It's always best when you can advocate with others since it strengthens causes, and resources can be shared at times. Search for good allies that may include people from outside the people you know. Alliances can be formed on common shared interests, or coalitions on temporary alliances. Collaborations are more 21st century where advocates learn and work together. Make tough decisions to work with allies who have common interests so relationships can form. But don't get bogged down with too many differences.

No matter which type of working together you choose, ask important questions to make sure that this is a good fit for you and your organization:
- Does their mission align with your cause and the results you seek?
- Would your group and others who share joint problems be helped by their mission?
- Do they have direct experiences or indirect conversations?
- Would it make a difference if this group is involved?
- Will the topic energize more networks or close some of them?

Community organizing differs from any parent involvement or engagement you've done. If unsure how to start organizing with others, begin by gaining needed skills as a school advocate. Read *Transforming Schools through Community Organizing: A Research Review.* In that step-by-step plan for organizing parents and others, you'll find information on many topics. Though it's written for schools, the information may be useful in starting your group.

One sensitive topic when dealing with systemic and individual racism is that of the support of European Americans with African Americans, called *allyship*. When looking at the South African anti-apartheid movement that utilized the support of white people, four lessons were learned. Use privilege to support the oppressed; those with privilege should educate others of privilege. The privileged can become activists alongside others. The last point is that the privileged should not expect to be leaders of the struggle and should not be decision makers, but supporters. (Fleischman and Graham).

Justice is related to actions and accountability.
--Naba'a Muhammad

Grassroots are common or ordinary people who differ from the elite or leadership of already established organizations. If you prefer to work with a grassroots organization, you will first need to find them on-line or ask others in the community. Or you may need to start a grassroots organization with others or strengthen an existing one, if needed. See *GettingSmart*.com for a list of *50 advocacy organizations* on their Smart List that includes equity advocates, personalized and competency-based learning advocates, policy advisors and resources and state advocacy organizations.

Never doubt
that a small group of thoughtful committed citizens
can change the world:
Indeed, it's the only thing that ever has.
--Margret Mead

Resources for Community Advocacy

1. Advocating for Change https://ctb.ku.edu/en/advocating-change
2. Advocating for Policy Change https://prosperitynow.org/putting-prosperity-within-reach-how-do-i-advocate-for-policy-change
3. Advocacy for change in Juvenile Justice https://www.aecf.org/blog/get-involved-advocates-for-change-in-juvenile-justice/
4. Racial equity tools ttps://www.racialequitytools.org/act/strategies/advocacy
5. Climate Change and Justice for George Floyd https://insideclimatenews.org/news/02062020/george-floyd-racial-justice-police-brutality-environment-climate-activism/
6. Creating a New Era of Public Safety https://civilrights.org/edfund/creating-a-new-era-of-public-safety/
7. The Top 10 Solutions to Cut Poverty and Grow the Middle Class https://www.americanprogress.org/issues/poverty/news/2014/09/17/9728 7/the-top-10-solutions-to-cut-poverty-and-grow-the-middle-class/

8. Sustainable Development Goals: Goal 1: End poverty in all its forms everywhere. https://www.un.org/sustainabledevelopment/poverty/

9. Policies to reduce poverty. https://www.economicshelp.org/macroeconomics/inequality/policies_reduce_poverty/
https://www.startups.com/library/expert-advice/small-business-grants-for-immigrants-and-minorities

10. https://blacklivesmatter.com/what-we-believe/

11. https://www.npr.org/2020/07/11/890000800/how-white-people-can-advocate-for-the-black-lives-matter-movement

12. Black Lives Matter: four lessons in white allyship from the South African anti-apartheid movement. The conversation.com – Leonie Fleischmann and Matthew Graham

13. https://www.forbes.com/sites/ericmosley/2019/10/17/how-to-create-a-more-inclusive-workplace-culture/#65e0e36d67bd

Advocacy Resources for Better Schools.

Since schools – or the learning received from them – can be problematic according to where you live, who you are racially or ethnically, or due to a lack of diversity in your workplace, you may want to advocate for better schools. The money we're able to earn to support our families for financial security is dependent on the education received when in schools, usually. You can teach yourself, as many African Americans had to do before schools were available in their areas, according to where they lived.

Advocate for good schools that all children deserve by sharing the following resources are aligned with school issues. The resources are for local school boards, schools and teachers. Use this information as you advocate for improved education and schools, but also use resources to support your cause. Do your research, then discuss with other advocates to determine changes that may be needed in your situation.

To learn more about other points important in advocating for better schools, contact Dr. Mapp for information from her dissertation on Teachers' Sense of Efficacy and African American Student Engagement. She developed lists explaining what to look for in Teacher Self-Efficacy, Culturally Responsive Pedagogy, Classroom Observation Checklists, etc.

I believe that education is the civil rights issue of our generation.
And if you care about promoting opportunity
and reducing inequality, the classroom is the place to start.

Great teaching is about so much more than education;
it is a daily fight for social justice.
---Arne Duncan

School Systems are usually directed by local boards of education under superintendents who may work on behalf of the board. They are supposed to look out for all students and elicit opinions from the community since they spend taxpayer funds. They need to promote diversity to benefit all students while supporting diverse school staffs. This information is useful in workplaces, also.

1. View a 12-minute TED Talk, *Changing Education Paradigms*, for Ken Burn's interpretation as to why U.S. schools need to be redesigned.

2. Sensitive issues may need to be tackled in private to process possibilities for change, like *Understanding White Privilege* (Kendall, 2001); Social Work Today - *Confronting the White Elephant* by Brittany Alafaro. Then discuss with mixed groups how the information should be applied.

3. See the *Taking Action Against Racism* website to help educators, families and others deal with understanding and moving beyond white privilege.

4. For businesses to better support parents, read and use *Your Workplace: Simple Investment, Big Reward.* Search Institute.

Schools must help students prepare for 21ˢᵗ century opportunities and challenges. Along with families, they should help students develop civically, emotionally, cognitively, vocationally and socially so they are ready for college, jobs, careers, citizenship, entrepreneurship and life.

1. See...*What Does an Equitable Classroom Look Like?*

2. A *chart* that can help youth after community violence occurs.

3. *Teaching in the Time of Trump* (Vol.31, No 3, Spring 2017); Ben Justice.

4. Check out a pdf for people skills that are also needed at work (Jacquelyn Smith, Forbes Staff).

5. Schools and businesses have to build trust; engage in cultural competency; confront social dominance and social justice; transform instructional practices and engage the entire school. (Howard, ASCD. *As Diversity Grows, So Must We*).

Dr. Martin Luther King, Jr. wrote about the future of our nation in 1967 and his ...   ... *thoughts, plans, and dreams for America's future,*
including the need for better jobs, higher wages,
decent housing, and quality education.
With a universal message of hope that continues to resonate,
King demanded an end to global suffering,
asserting that humankind-for the first time-
has the resources and technology to eradicate poverty.
From a review of *Where Do We Go from Here? Chaos or Community?*

It is now five decades later and time for each of us to consider why things haven't changed. After going through this book and the pandemics, most readers now know that each of us has a responsibility to improve ourselves so that collectively, we can improve our nation. If America can do this, any country in the world can. Ask yourself this important question for your next steps!

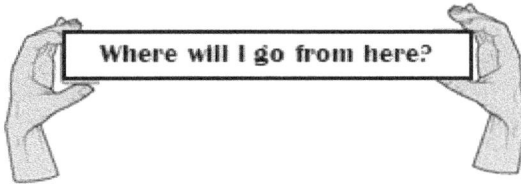

Where will I go from here?

If we are to have peace on earth...
our loyalties must transcend
our race, our tribe, our class, and our nation,
and this means
we must develop
a world perspective.
–Dr. Martin Luther King, Jr.

You
must be the change
you
want to see in the world.
–Mahatma Gandhi

Conclusion

It's hoped that this book assisted you in not just knowing what to do to make sense of today. Its goal was to support you as you pulled forth the will, courage and commitment to take the initiative to act to improve your human connections with others. A review of the major clues introduced in this book are noted here for your empowerment and transformation:

1. ***Many decisions and choices*** made today are based in our pasts and have consequences for the future. Everything is connected, affecting other things that happen, since nothing is isolated. We can't predict and control what's going to happen so we need to be aware of possible consequences for our decisions. We need to use wisdom, faith, discernment, updated knowledge, skills and attitude shifts for best outcomes.

2. ***Continuous learning*** is needed throughout our lifetimes to keep up with the constant changes in life, society, other nations and our Earth that affect humanity. We need to be creative, innovative and open to change. We need to feel what's happening around us while thinking on different levels to gain solutions to complex problems. When working with others, we need to understand more about our personal selves and each other, with clear communication skills, empathy, social and emotional skills, civility and respect.

3. ***Positive relationships*** are needed since we are all human and need to be humane with each other as we influence, solve problems together and repair our democracy. This begins with the healing of our personal selves, our families and neighbors, people from other cultures, work, institutions like schools and government, and people from other cultures. Then we can work globally to resolve our shared Earth and Peace issues.

4. ***Be positive*** to attract more good things into your life through wiser decisions and attitudes. Think deeper as you examine yourself, learn to think critically, be capable, flexible and accountable while learning soft skills, social responsibility, ethics and leadership to share with others.

5. ***Literacy changes*** as societies change and we have to be flexible enough to accept change as it happens. Literacy changes influence our health and environment, global awareness and our finances. We need to become more literate in economics and business; entrepreneurship and citizenship; information, media and technology. Change is here and we have to adapt, disrupt and transform to improve our situations, or we will destroy ourselves.

We Have to Be More Humane for HUMANITY's Sake
since our Democracy and Earth
are on shaky ground!

The decade of the 2020s is Pivotal as
Choices Are Made to Develop and Use
Our Will, Strength, Courage and Commitment
to do what's Necessary to
Make Sense of Today
so We Choose to Do and Be Better for Future Generations!

First, they came for the _____ [fill in the blank with who you don't like]
and I did not speak out because I was not a _____.
Then they came for the [other group I don't like] _____
and I did not speak out because I was not a _____........
[continue for every group in our nation you have a problem with]
Then they came for me—
and there was no one left to speak for me.
-- Martin Niemoller

Will this be the history of Our United States of America?

Selected References and End Notes

Boggs, G.L. and J. (1993). *Revolution and Evolution in the 20th Century.*

DeAngelis, B. (1994). *Real Moments.* Esp. Ch 2: Crisis of Spirit in America.

Duvall, B. (2019). *The Martin Family Legacy: There Is Always Room for One More... Lourenza, Finis, Herbert and Howitt.* (maternal family)

Embry, I. A. (2014). *Balancing the Rift: Reconnectualizing the Pasenture.*

Embry, O. N. (2013). *Expanding Horizons Through Creative Expressions.*

Kurashige, S. & Boggs, G. L. (2012). *The Next American Revolution: Sustainable Activism for the Twenty-First Century.* U of California.

Mapp, D.L'T., (2019*). Our Children and Future: Lessons in Family and School Engagement (2nd ed.). SAUCE Series.*

Mapp, D.L'T., (2020*). Making Sense of Today for Better Connections Tomorrow (2nd ed., Vol. 1) SAUCE Series.*

Mapp, D.L'T., (2021). *My Child, Our Future (2nd ed., Vol. 2).* Also available in a Spiral-bound Guided Journal: *Prepare Our Children...*

Mapp, J.R. (2017). *Chance or Circumstance: A Memoir and Journey through the Struggle for Civil Rights.* Jamesrmapp.org/Audio also

Menkart, D., Murray, A.D., and View, J. L., Eds. (2004). *Putting the Movement Back into Civil Rights Teaching: A Resource Guide.*

National Governors Association Center for Best Practices, Council Chief State School Officers. (2010). *Common Core State Standards.* Washington DC: National Governors Association Center for Best Practices, Council of Chief State School Officers.

Quisenberry, R.L. (2002). *A Saga of the Black Man* plus other dualities.

Singh, A. A. (2019). *The Racial Healing Handbook: Practical Activities to Help You Challenge Privilege, Confront Systemic Racism & Engage in Collective Healing.* The Social Justice Handbook Series.

Snyder, K.J., Acker-Hocevarl, M., and Snyder, K.R. (2000). *Living on the Edge of Chaos: Leading Schools into the Global Age.* ASQ Quality.

Takaki, R. (1993). *A Different Mirror: A History of Multicultural America.* Read Chapter 1 at the least though the whole book will open your world.

Yes! Magazine and other media to do and be better: *The Crisis Magazine*; *Mother Jones*; *Mother Earth News; Black Enterprise; DiversityInc Magazine; The Call, The Griot; Teaching for Change; Black Financial Channel; Rethinking Schools; Earth Day.org, etc.*

Following are abbreviated **End-Notes** (on-line and print) that are not in order and not always complete. Place the partial link or title in your favorite browser or check schoolingsolutions.com website for direct links to sites.

PART I: What's Needed to Make Sense?

1. *Use Story to Heal Our Nation* . Psychology Today.com. blog 2016
2. *How Your life Story Can Help You Succeed in Life and Work*. Nbcnews.com NCNA. Or *How to Make Sense of Any Mess* by Abby Covert.
3. *Step by step to build community*. Community Tool Box, KU edu
4. *American Medical Association*. November 26 Report.
5. Blanchard, *Leadership and One Minute Manager*. Review/summary
6. https://www.weforum.org/agenda/2020/06/theres-nothing-new-about-this-new-normal-heres-why/
7. Chime Asonye, 05 June 2020
8. https://www.prb.org/americanattitudesaboutpovertyandthepoor/
9. ://www.pewresearch.org/fact-tank/2017/10/30/global-views-political-systems/
10. Learn more at roots of action com critical-thinking

Part II: The Personal Becomes Political

11. Anderson, Claud. *A Black History Reader.* Poweronomics.com
12. We are beloved org- a new ecosystem to sustain equitable diverse schools
13. Gcorr org., 25 traits of the beloved community
14. Howard Zinn, *A People's History of the United States*
15. *How do you respond to racism?* Oregon Center for Educational Equity
16. https://ucanr.edu/blogs/blogcore/postdetail.cfm?postnum=21460
17. Business inside com myths about American history
18. https://www.showingupforracialjustice.org/white-supremacy-culture.html
19. https://www.npr.org/2020/06/09/873054935/want-to-have-better-conversations-about-racism-with-your-parents-heres-
20. A Decade of Watching Black People Die, Code Switch. NPR.
21. Interaction Institute for Social Change. *Exploring Racial Identity Agenda: Stages of Racial Identity Development.* RacialEquityTools.org.
22. Moore, Eddie. 21-Day Racial Equity [Habit] Building Challenge.
23. Smith, Jamil (2015). What Does Seeing Black Men Die Do...? New Republic
24. https://www.thelawofattraction.com/poverty-mindset-financial-abundance/
25. https://www.self.inc/blog/7-tips-for-breaking-the-cycle-of-poverty
https://www.creativespirits.info/resources/infographics/how-to-deal-with-racist-people
26. https://www.npr.org/2020/06/09/873054935/want-to-have-better-conversations-about-racism-with-your-parents-heres-how
27. https://www.cnn.com/2020/06/04/health/how-to-be-an-anti-racist-wellness/index.html
28. https://www.cnn.com/audio/podcasts/don-lemon-silence-is-not-an-option?utm_source=bouncex_podcast_overlay
29. Survival skills https://www.survivalsullivan.com/urban-survival-skills-you-need-to-know/ and https://www.outdoorlife.com/story/hunting/outdoor-skills-

you-can-teach-your-child/   https://www.pblworks.org/what-is-pbl

30. Nikole Hannah-Jones (1619 Project) https://www.nytimes.com/
    interactive/2019/08/14/magazine/1619-america-slavery.html
31. //www.vox.com/identities/2019/8/26/20829771/slavery-textbooks-history
32. Saad, Layla (2014). Me and White Supremacy Workbook. *Telling Our Own Story*. Perception.org 2014
33. Village of Wisdom, I Thought We Were White? Multiracial in America... (pew social trends org); Raising Biracial (race relations about com); 6 things (vox com biracial). Adopted point of view (the root com black adoptees)
34. https://www.healthypeople.gov/2020/topics-objectives/topic/social-determinants-health/interventions-resources/discrimination
35. ACT-Youth for Ethnic and Racial Identity Development. See a YouTube video on "Why All the Black Kids Sitting Together in the Cafeteria?" J. Keitt.
36. Read a Food Label? at live strong com; natural/organic –naturally savvy dot
37. "Menu Planning: save Time-organized home.com; Eating Well: Healthy Recipes & Cookinglight.com for "Healthy Recipes, Nutrition Tips & Guides"
38. " 10 Ways To Quit Your Worst at Prevention com and See rd com /health/
39. "Why Are Americans Obese?" for video at public health
40. *Teaching Tolerance*, a free magazine sent to schools three times a year.
41. Find Fed Up dot com documentary on foods in the US
42. "What Screen Time Really Does to Kids' Brains at psychology today com
43. "Teens and Sleep" sleep foundation org and How Much? Web md com
44. See the vimeo "10 Steps to Get Home Safely!" when confronted by police
45. Other issues: money how stuff works com/personal-finance/college
46. See literacy net org parents/
47. See Roots of Action com for newsletter, free e-book
48. See school family com blog 2015/05/12/
49. Meyerson, C. the nation. com time Americans ..true history racial oppression
50. R. Weingarten. *The true story of public education in America*
51. U.S. Census Bureau. Census dot gov
52. 1 in 5 US moms have kids with multiple dads, study says at nbcnews.com
53. Roehlkepartain, (Nov 2019), Reframing Adult Youth Partnerships.search-

Part III: Schooling, Quality of Life and other information

54. America's Families and Living Arrangements: 2012 census.gov 2013
55. Childhood Emotional Neglect World of Psychology-psychcentral dotcom
56. Body Image and Self-Esteem at kidshealth dot org
57. Child Mind Institute Empowering Change resources at childmind dot org
58. National Responsible Fatherhood Clearinghouse Look at fatherhood dot gov
59. A silent crisis in men's health gets worse. Tara Parker-Pope; Caitlin Gilbert
60. View a video on... Become Better Dads at nationswell dot .com
61. Children of Incarcerated Parent challenges at youth dot gov; aecf dot org
62. Effect of Divorce: What Makes a Difference," extension dot purdue dot edu
63. Nat. Fatherhood Initiative Absence Crisis at fatherhood org : See websites for Fathers Inc. & Honorable Men; sign up for 3x week blog at family first. net
64. Test Yourself for Hidden Bias, Tolerance org and act foryouth dot net. Blind spot: Washington post dot com; see tolerance dot org
65. depts.washington.edu/fammed/wp-content/uploads Cycle_ofSocializationHandout.pdf

66. Act for youth net for information on adolescence identity
67. Mapp unpublished dissertation: Teachers Sense of Efficacy and African American Student Engagement: A Case Study of a Kentucky Middle School.
68. Art of manliness com/ old fashioned but good info; psychology ext. colo stat
69. See great schools.org/g k/articles/take-great-notes/ note taking clues.
70. See we are teachers.com and See wiki how.com
71. See treasury direct gov.com and earn more at dwiki how com/ pay attention
72. drug free org know .child using/get help/child need help/
73. See great schools.org for more on discipline.
74. See family findlaw com
75. Check out ext colo state edu /pubs / consumer for more information.
76. A study sheet is located at pcsd org Community/
77. See us new com… 529 boost
78. See the 10 themes of National Curriculum Standards for Social Studies.org
79. See Danica McKellar (actress and mathematician) with her books for 5th- 12th grade girls and Monster Math for boys are located on line
80. See *10 Actions for Bullied* online at education.com and find 03/14/12.
81. https://depts.washington.edu/geograph/diversity/HarroCofS.pdf
82. To prepare: ted.com/conversations 18180; late com articles/life education/14.03   Firestone, Lisa – *Psychology Today*, 7 Ways to Stop Viol
83. Email Dr. Mapp for multiplication tables/math facts/$1 for 2, leave phone #.
84. Check out your free career test com
85. If you've run out of ideas, see middle earth n j dot word
86. Check out futurist speaker com/2014/03/ 162-future-jobs
87. For tech help certification see career advice monster com/ job-search.
88. See my college guide org/articles/9/159/engineers
89. See money cnn com/ 2013/10/30
90. Prayers for special help com/ serenity-prayer.html
91. *The Social Studies wars, Now and Then.* Read it Ronald W. Evans or listen to it at Visions of Ed episode 40.
92. Rosario, I. (June 6, 2020).. *This List of Books, Films and Podcasts About Racism is a Start, Not A Panacea.* Codeswitch, NPR
93. https://www.psychologytoday.com/us/blog/mindful-anger/201804/9-steps-healing-childhood-trauma-adult
94. Morris, Monique. (2016). *Pushout: The Criminalization of Black Girls ....*
95. McCammon, Sarah (June 15, 2020) *Want to Have Better Conversations About Racism With Your Parents? Here's How.* Life Kit, NPR.
96. https://www.entrepreneur.com/article/288340 Article on empowerment.
97. https://www.bbc.com/news/science-environment-53100800 Greta Thunberg: Climate change 'as urgent' as coronavirus
98. Learn how to start your own business https://www.entrepreneur.com/article/269771
99. NPR. (April 26, 2019). *Talking Race with Young Children. Parenting: Difficult Conversations.* (20 minute listen)
100. Shapiro, Ari. (June 9, 2020). *There Is No Neutral': 'Nice White People' Can Still Be Complicit In A Racist Society.* All Things Considered, NPR
101. 2019 Year Ender: Climate Crisis with the end of the hottest decade
102. https://news.harvard.edu/gazette/story/2018/04/less-stress-clearer-thoughts-with-mindfulness-meditation/
103. https://www.fundera.com/blog/best-small-business-loans-grants-immigrants.

104. Gilligan, J. *Violence: Reflections on a National Epidemic*
105. https://www.racialequitytools.org/resourcefiles/Compilation_of_Racial_Identit
y_Models_7_15_11.pdf
106. https://www.youtube.com/watch?v=-ase16a3VrQ Peace treaty now?

*You're at the End of This Book
Today -
Hopefully it Helped You
to Make Sense of our Past and Present
for A Better
Tomorrow!*

< A Note from Dr. Mapp on the Schooling Solutions You Seek >

Hopefully you checked out some of the sites in this section of the book. Your group may want to contract with Dr. Mapp for professional development. >< Newer research has its advantages at times, but we have to make sure that original documents used as foundational to today's research is really understood by today's researchers. I realized when writing my dissertation that original documents sometimes contain the context from the past that may still be in operation today in education and in our families. ><We can't assume that problems today are different from the past because of connections to larger issues. Technology's use does not make us more capable since digitized work is only as good and useful as the understanding of the program's developer. Technology – and AI – are just tools after all, not people.

We Can Do Better
So Next Generations are Better Prepared for the Future World
They Will Inherit – IF We Choose To!

*Thank You For Joining Us on this Journey to
Make Sense of Today
while Considering Next Steps to
Uplift Humanity,
Save our Earth
and our Democracy!*

Be Safe and Well - and Understand that We're All in This Together!
Dr. DeBora L.T. Mapp
Schooling Solutions LLC

About the Author

DeBora L'T. Mapp, EdD, is a retired educator, consultant and author with Schooling Solutions LLC, a KY certified MWBE firm. At an early age she developed a holistic point of view that opened her to being different. Descended from an enslaved ancestor who bought himself and his wife out of slavery, she is a granddaughter of farmers, daughter of civil rights activists, one of eight children and member of a large extended legacy farm family. She attended good, segregated schools in an all-Black southern world until her last two years at the desegregated "home of the rebels." After graduation she attended a predominantly white university.

In college, Dr. Mapp went through a conscious metamorphosis before becoming a teacher in desegregated settings. She served with social justice change agent skills to facilitate changed opinions and improved performances in positions that ended with higher education as a professor and earlier administrator of a First-Year counseling unit; to a public school district curriculum coordinator and schoolteacher-leader; to community agencies as a career counselor and teacher of four-year-olds. It took her 13 years to earn a doctorate, but she parented one daughter and four sons to engineering degrees during that time. She became an entrepreneur after being laid off three times in three years. Dr. Mapp's family, work experience and research helped her to understand that living, learning, schooling and our families are linked and impacted by historical, political, educational and social forces that require holistic approaches for better outcomes. It made sense for her to do so!

"My former husband and I intentionally made plans and decisions about our children's upbringing, rather than leaving things to chance. We were aware of our personal and collective histories and sought to make sense of the times to link home learnings and community experiences with schooling. I constantly researched wise practices to learn more about my culture, our children, our community, my students and work positions with wellness and well-being.
    As a public-school teacher, I was reluctant even to consider private school until I visited a Montessori school which was a good fit for our family until the oldest were ready for public middle school. The oldest three were old school and easily prepared for the world and our twins were new school and took years to launch, but we did it! Married for two decades, their father and I divorced but we put our children on the right paths as they planned for their futures. All of them are caring, smart, well-rounded and critical thinking adults who understand the importance of family, faith and caring for people and the Earth with 4 in-laws and 7 smart, amazing, thriving, beautiful grandchildren."

With this guidebook, you will make sense of your life, too!

Schooling Solutions Logo & Framework

The West African Adinkra stylized heart symbol, *Sankofa*, presents the importance of bringing wise knowledge and practices from the past into the present to make positive future progress. Our logo is a stylized apple/heart/Sankofa shape representing education, love and caring, with green leaves representing development and life. The healing hands with an indigo background honor Our Ancestors. The Sankofa bird on the cover is the other representation of Sankofa.

S.A.U.C.E. is the Framework developed by Dr. Mapp so More People can begin to **Speak** and **Act** on usually **Unspoken Connections** to **Embrace** needed changes more confidently.

Ideas were started with her Case Study Dissertation on Teachers' Sense of Efficacy and African American Student Engagement

The sought result is more 21st Century Adults ready to Assist Next Generations in meeting the complex challenges and opportunities of the future world they will inherit.

< The SAUCE Series Includes Books and E-Books: >

1..YOU ARE YOUR CHILD'S BEST TEACHER:
Intentionally Linking Home and School © 2012   40 Page Booklet

2..YOU ARE YOUR CHILD'S BEST TEACHER:
A Holistic Guide to Link Home and School © 2015 (1st ed.)

3..OUR CHILDREN AND FUTURE: :   *(Especially for Educators)*
Lessons in Family and School Engagement © 2019 (*2nd ed.*)

<Books 4, 5 and 6 are Excerpted from the 2nd Edition with 2023 Updates>

4..MAKING SENSE OF TODAY   © 2020
FOR BETTER CONNECTIONS TOMORROW (2nd ed., Vol. 1)

5..MY CHILD, OUR FUTURE   *(2nd ed., Vol. 2)* © 2021

6..PREPARE OUR CHILDREN GUIDED JOURNAL/BOOK © 2021

7..CHOOSE PURPOSE OVER FEAR, WIN EVERY TIME
Success Edition Anthology © 2022

Tired of the same results? Try Schooling Solutions!

Audience

To better prepare Our Children (Next Generations)
for success in the future world they will inherit,
our ideal clients are Parents/Families as children's first teachers,
Young Adults preparing for adulting and
school and community Teachers and Mentors who are all
ready to update their skills, attitudes and knowledge beyond tech
for a futures orientation.
#Ready2Inherit #MakingSenseofToday #MyChildOurFuture

**Contact Dr. Mapp for A Different Perspective – it may be
what your group needs to Shift Actions for Real Change!**

Webinars, Workshops and Speaking Engagements
(Remote and at Your Locale)
Books, Greeting Cards, Posters and Other Resources
Gift Certificates and Consultations
with S.A.U.C.E.

+ Custom Topics to Align with Your Occasion
+ Parenting Workshops for Well-being and Home-Learning
+ Resources for Home Schooling Families
+ Support for Home Schools and New Teachers
+ Workshops, Professional & Staff Development on Book Topics

**Dr. DeBora L'T. Mapp
Schooling Solutions LLC
835 S. 7th St. #802
Louisville, KY 40203-0802**

Phone/Text 502.317.2627
Email: Support@DrMappSpeaks.com or edcconsult@gmail.com
Author Website: https://www.DrMappSpeaks.com

**<Buy Books from Website, Amazon.com, Lulu.com (POD),
Global Distribution, Barnes &Nobles or Ask at Local Bookstore>**

**Also Contact Dr. Mapp for <Book Discounts for Large Groups>
<Speaking, PD & Webinars> <eBooks> <P.O. Invoices>
and < for Possible Translations into Other Languages>**

Notes

Notes

www.ingramcontent.com/pod-product-compliance
Lightning Source LLC
Chambersburg PA
CBHW032105080426

42733CB00006B/428